DATE DUE

the search for Life

Thomas G. Aylesworth

*Illustrated with
photographs and drawings*

Rand McNally & Company
Chicago / New York / San Francisco

FOR JIM AND JO RAWLINGS

WHO KNOW ABOUT HOSPITALS

Library of Congress Cataloging in Publication Data

Aylesworth, Thomas G.
    The search for life.
    SUMMARY: Examines, both in scientific and ethical
terms, genetic research, experiments in freezing, the
development of artificial body parts, and progress in
transplanting human organs.
    1. Medicine—Juvenile literature. 2. Human biology—
Juvenile literature. 3. Medical ethics—Juvenile
literature. [1. Medicine. 2. Medical ethics] I. Title.
R 130.5 A9
ISBN 0-528-82144-X
ISBN 0-528-80148-1 (lib. bdg.)

Jacket illustration by Bill Chambers

Some of the material in Chapter 1 has appeared in different
form in *The Alchemists: Magic Into Science,* Text Copyright
© 1973 by Thomas G. Aylesworth. Illustrations Copyright © 1973
by Addison-Wesley Publishing Co., Inc.

First Printing, 1975

Contents

Acknowledgments

I am deeply indebted to the following people, institutions, and industries, who gave me so much help: the American Heart Association; Bonnie Baggett of ILC Dover; Dr. Roy E. Cameron of Darwin Research Institute; Dr. John Charnley of Wrightington Hospital; Edward O. Ethell of the Ear Research Institute; Dr. Robert H. Foote of Cornell University; Evelyn Goodwin of State University of New York Downstate Medical Center; Dr. E. F. Graham of the University of Minnesota; Georgia A. Herbert of the University of Florida; Jeremy Heymsfeld of SmithKline Corporation; Gene Medford of General Electric; National Institutes of Health; Richard Newhall of Clemson University; John Rozier of Emory University; Dr. George E. Seidel, Jr., of Colorado State University; A. B. Stakemire of the Agricultural Research Council; and Susan B. Stockman of The Children's Hospital Medical Center, Boston.

Permission for the use of photographs was given by the following persons, institutions, and industries: page 28 from the National Aeronautics and Space Administration; page 50 from ILC Dover; page 58 (drawing by Michael O'Mara) from the Ear Research Institute; page 61 (top) from the National Institutes of Health; pages 61 (bottom) and 76 (Emerich C. Gross, photographer) from the American Heart Association; pages 88 and 89 from The Children's Hospital Medical Center; page 92 (Tracy O'Neal, photographer) from Emory University; pages 100 and 101 based on drawings by Virginia Aylesworth.

Quotations from Jean Rostand's *Man of Tomorrow*, copyright 1966 by Doubleday & Co., reprinted with thanks to Doubleday & Co. Quotation from Charles Finney's *The Circus of Dr. Lao*, copyright 1935 by Viking Press, reprinted courtesy of Barthold Fles.

Illustrations

The Ancient Search

Most people have heard of Ponce de León and his search for a fountain of youth. And everyone knows about the Frankenstein monster. We have all heard that a cat has nine lives. But what do these three things have in common? The fact that they are talked about. These stories are told and retold because we are all curious about how to live longer. We would even like to discover the secret of life itself.

Today, medical programs have a high rating on television. Marcus Welby constantly fights disease. The Six-Million-Dollar Man is a triumph of spare-part surgery. In the bookstores, some of the most popular volumes are concerned with human aging and the struggle to prolong life. Scientists travel to far-off Russia and South America to study groups of people who typically live long lives.

But the alchemists started the search centuries ago.

The alchemists were really the first people who tried to discover scientific facts in their laboratories. Of course, there had been a few experimental scientists in Greece, Arabia, China, India, and other places before the alchemists came on the scene, but not many.

Most people have heard that the alchemists were always looking for a way to turn base metals such as lead, mercury, and iron into gold. Many alchemists felt that the best way to do this was to experiment until they found the *philosopher's stone*, a magic substance that would do the job.

But why were they looking for gold? The importance of gold goes back a long way. This metal was first found in the ancient land of Nubia, more than five thousand years ago. The people living there thought that gold was a part of the sun that had come down to earth. Since they believed that the sun was a god, the metal was considered holy, too. Add to this the fact that gold does not tarnish or rust, and it is small wonder that people believed that it was the most perfect of metals. When the Egyptians ruled this part of the earth, they accepted the idea that gold was holy and decided that it should be reserved for the use of the pharaoh, since he also was holy.

Most alchemists worthy of the name were not looking for gold just to make themselves wealthy. In a way, these men were both scientists and philosophers. And although we may look at their work as part religion and part science, they did not separate it in that way. They thought that by practicing their scientific art they could perfect themselves as human beings and, at the same time, perfect metals by turning them into gold.

Of course, the alchemists never found the philosopher's stone, but along the way they discovered many other things. They discovered chemicals that we use today in dyes, varnish, medicine, and steel. They developed waterproofing for leather and cloth, rust inhibitors, luminous ink, smelling salts, sleeping potions, new kinds of explosives, and drugs that could be used to fight pain.

You might wonder who could possibly believe in a substance that could change other material into gold. But it is not as strange as it seems. These men knew nothing about atoms and molecules. Today we know that many substances can change into other substances. Over a period of many years, for example, radioactive radium will turn into lead.

We also know that scientists can change one element into another. In 1970, a team of scientists, at the University of California in Berkeley, created an isotope of a new element, element 105, and suggested that it be called *hahnium*. Isotopes of an element have a different number of neutrons in their nuclei, but the same number of protons as the element. At about the same time, a group of Russian scientists created a different isotope of element 105 which they proposed to call *nielsbohrium*, after the Danish physicist who theorized about the structure of the atom. Credit for the discovery has not yet been determined.

This element had never existed before. The Americans had manufactured its isotope by bombarding another element, californium 249, with nitrogen ions. Each californium atom picked up a nitrogen nucleus and gave off four neutrons.

But think. This is very sophisticated science. However, isn't it what the alchemists were trying to do? Perhaps the early scientists just didn't have enough equipment or modern knowledge to accomplish their goals.

Creating gold from base metals was not all that the alchemists were trying to do. Many of them were looking for a substance called the *elixir of life*. They thought that the elixir, like the philosopher's stone, was a substance that would remove impurities from the human body. Some people believed that the philosopher's stone and the elixir of life were the same thing.

Roger Bacon, the great English philosopher and scientist, also looked for the elixir of life. As a matter of fact, he once wrote down a formula for it:

> A substance annealed in the fourth degree and floating in the sea.
>
> A substance floating in the air and washed ashore by the sea.
>
> A substance planted in India and found in the entrails of very old animals.
>
> Two serpents that serve as food to the inhabitants of Tyre and Ethiopia.

That does sound like a strange formula, and it would be impossible to follow it in a laboratory. But that is the way the alchemists often wrote up their findings. And there were several reasons for making these writings as mysterious as possible.

First of all, the alchemists were worried about some of the rulers who were in power. The potentates of the day held all of the cards. They could throw an alchemist into prison to force him to give up his secrets about the philosopher's stone or the elixir of life. If this happened, the alchemist might give the king a strange-sounding formula and let his own wise men try to interpret it.

Then there were the leaders of the churches. Some of them believed that the alchemists were trying to make men more perfect by developing magic potions to prolong life.

This, of course, was true—the alchemists *were* looking for ways to achieve human perfection. But these church people felt that the perfection of humans was their work, and their work alone. No one but the church should have anything to do with that, so they tried to stop the alchemists' work.

It should be pointed out that these national and religious leaders were European, Near Eastern, and Far Eastern. No one nationality or sect can possibly be singled out.

Finally, the alchemists were afraid of all the greedy people in the world who might want to steal their secrets. In the fifteenth century, Thomas Norton, an alchemist, wrote this poem:

> This art must ever secret be,
> The cause whereof is this, as ye may see:
> If one evil man has thereof all his will,
> All Christian peace he might easily spill,
> And with his pride he might pull down
> Rightful kings and princes of renown.

So the alchemists wrote their formulas in a symbolic language that only other alchemists could understand.

At first, the elixir of life was thought of as a magical potion that could prolong life, cure disease, and turn base metals into gold. But after a time, alchemists began to believe that the elixir was merely a substance that could help people live longer and more healthy lives.

One of the recipes for the elixir was written down by a seventeenth-century alchemist, the Frenchman, Jean d'Espagnet:

> Take three parts of red earth [the philosopher's stone],
> and air, six parts altogether, mix them thoroughly and pre-
> pare a metallic paste like butter in which the earth can no

longer be felt with the finger. Add one and a half parts of fire and place it in a thoroughly closed vessel and give it fire of the first degree for digestion. Then you prepare an extract of the elements according to the degrees of the fire until they are reduced to a solid earth. The matter becomes like a shining, translucent red stone and then it is ready. Put it into a pot on a modest fire and moisten it by its oil, drop by drop, until it becomes fluent without smoke. Do not be afraid that the mercury will vaporize; the earth drinks the humidity eagerly, because it is a part of its nature. Now you have the elixir ready. Thank God for His grace that He has granted you, use it for His praise and keep the secret.

Another early formula for the preparation of the elixir of life mixed eight pounds of sugar of mercury with a piece of the philosopher's stone. Of course, there was no place to find the ingredients.

Johann Trithemius, another alchemist, suggested a mixture of calomel, gentian, cinnamon, aniseed, nard (an ancient ointment made from a plant known as spikenard), coral, tartar, and mace. It was to be dissolved in bromium and drunk twice a day, morning and night, for a month. In the second month, it was to be drunk only in the morning. After that the dosage was to be reduced to three times per week. But it was to be continued for life.

One of the most intriguing formulas, written in alchemists' language, was this one:

Ten parts of coelestiall slime; separate the male from the female, and each afterwards from its own earth, physically, mark you, and with no violence. Conjoin after separation in due, harmonic vital proportion; and straightway, the Soul descending from the pyroplastic sphere, shall restore, by a mirific embrace, its dead and deserted body. Proceed according to the Volcanico magica theory, till they are exalted into the Fifth Metaphysical Rota. This is that world-renowned medicine, whereof so many have scribbled, which, notwithstanding, so few have known.

The alchemists never did find this magical substance, of course. A single medicine that could cure all ailments could not possibly exist. But who is to say that they wasted their time looking for it? They laid the groundwork for many of today's medical discoveries. They were trying to prolong life by looking for beneficial medicines, just as Jonas Salk was when he was developing the polio vaccine, and just as Alexander Fleming was when he was discovering the effects of penicillin. The alchemists made many mistakes, but the greatest of these scientists made significant and long-lasting contributions to the development of science and medicine.

Some people say that Arnold of Villanova was the first genuine alchemist. He was born in Spain in 1235. After setting up his doctor's office in Barcelona, he wrote books on health care, medical cures, epilepsy, gallstones, and gout. Arnold was also a believer in astrology and numerology. It is said that he might delay the beginning of a scientific investigation if the influences of the stars and numbers were not right. This may have affected the accuracy of his experiments.

He also mixed a great deal of sorcery in his formulas. He advised that an emerald be hung around the neck of a newborn infant to prevent epilepsy. He recommended wearing a coral chain around the middle to guard against stomachaches. For sore feet he suggested tying frogs' legs, eagles' talons, or turtles' feet to your toes. And he warned that if you washed your hair too often or washed your eyes in cold water, you would go blind.

Arnold was always getting into trouble with the Church. Eventually, he was sentenced to be burned at the stake. The ending of his story sounds like a fairy tale. But it is said that while Arnold was waiting for his execution, Pope Boniface became ill. Arnold cured the pope and was appointed papal physician—the pope even gave him a free castle!

Then along came Paracelsus. Biochemist, surgeon, physician, magician, and alchemist—this was Paracelsus. He was one of the first to separate the folklore and witchcraft of the past from the body of knowledge that was to develop into modern medical science.

While searching for the truth he was ridiculed, taunted, and exiled. He was a man who said, "Medicine is not merely a science but an art. It does not consist in compounding pills and plasters and drugs of all kinds, but it deals with the processes of life. . . . The character of the physician may act more powerfully upon the patient than all the drugs employed."

This Swiss alchemist was born near Zurich in 1493, just a year after Columbus set sail on his first voyage. Although he was often called Theophrastus or Paracelsus, his real name was Philippus Aureolus Theophrastus Parcelsus Bombastus von Hohenheim.

When he was nine, he and his family moved to Carinthia, a region that is now a part of southern Austria, so that his father could open a medical practice. Later they moved to the village of Schwaz, in what is now western Austria, where his father became a mining engineer.

Paracelsus, the Swiss alchemist who revolutionized medicine.

This might seem unusual, but in Parcelsus's time there were many people who didn't know the difference between a physician and a metallurgist. One king commissioned a metal worker to dissect the body of a young woman to find out the cause of her death. "After all," he must have thought, "physicians and metallurgists are both scientists."

Most historians agree that Parcelsus never went to a university, but was taught by his father to be a physician.

This was not unusual either. In fact, through the nineteenth century, doctors on the American frontier did not always have training in medical schools. Often, they just studied with a physician, made house calls with him, read his books, and eventually, went out on their own to practice medicine.

Besides, medicine was not the most popular course of study at the universities in Paracelsus's time. The course was usually a series of lectures, spoken in Latin. There was very little laboratory work. The University of Heidelberg in Germany did not even get around to buying its first skeleton for study until the middle of the sixteenth century.

Paracelsus decided to toss away all of his medical books and develop his art by studying nature. But he also studied metallurgy and chemistry. These extra courses, plus the fact that his father had studied metals, were probably responsible for the fact that Paracelsus searched for medical cures in the metallic elements. For example, he was one of the very first to use mercury as a cure for syphilis, a treatment that was still being used in the nineteenth century.

Later in his life, Paracelsus settled for a time in Basel, Switzerland, where he was appointed to the faculty of the medical school.

He publicly burned some medical textbooks written by Galen and Avicenna, highly regarded physicians who were no longer living, saying that the books were worthless. This meant that he had turned his back on the medical establishment, for these were the approved texts at that time.

But perhaps his greatest crime, as far as his fellow professors were concerned, was that his class lectures were not given in Latin. He spoke to the students in German.

Paracelsus was not above getting information wherever he could. He consulted, as he said, "barbers, midwives, sorcerers, alchemists, in monasteries, among common people and nobles, from the wise and from the simpleminded."

The point is that he thought that all people were alchemists in one way or another. People who baked bread were alchemists because they had found the secret of wheat and yeast. A farmer growing crops was an alchemist because he had found the secret of water, soil, seeds, and weather.

Paracelsus's revolutionary ideas uncovered truths of which his contemporaries were totally unaware. He talked about the *sap of life,* and taught that this substance, blood, was very important to human health. And this was more than a century before it was discovered that blood circulated through the body.

He invented a new type of smelling salts and a sleeping potion. He learned of the importance of iron in our bodies. He was the first to use laudanum, an opium derivative, to kill pain. By the way, laudanum was the medical painkiller most often used up to the time of the American Civil War.

To be fair to his fellow professors, we must admit that Paracelsus was irritatingly arrogant. He wouldn't concede that any other physician had a valid point of view. On the other hand, maybe Paracelsus's colleagues were wrong. After all, he did cure people that others could not help. And he did look all over Europe for the elixir of life.

This great alchemist died in 1541.

Besides the elixir of life, many of the alchemists spent their time looking for a creature called the *homunculus.* The homunculus was supposed to be a little man who could be created in a flask by an alchemist. In short, he was a spark of life that was artificially created. Needless to say, they never found him, but it was not because they didn't try.

Although no one knows the precise origin of the homunculus legend, it was probably not invented by the alchemists. There was an ancient African superstition that if a drop of a woman's blood was placed in a pot and covered up for nine months, a child would then be found inside the pot. And for centuries, it was believed in Europe that every human sperm contained a homunculus that was ready for implantation and development inside the womb.

One of the first alchemic homunculus stories was told by an ancient practitioner, Zosimus. He was an Egyptian who lived during the fourth century A.D. Zosimus claimed that he had decided to be an alchemist because of a dream he had one night.

In his dream, he beheld an altar with a bottle on the top of it. A little copper-colored man escaped from the bottle, took a bath in a black liquid, and turned silver in color. Then he jumped into a fire. His eyes turned red, and his body became gold. This story was a combination of the legends about the philosopher's stone and the homunculus.

One of the greatest of the alchemists also believed in the homunculus. Albert von Bollstädt, better known as Albertus Magnus, was only a part-time scientist. Albertus was born in Germany in 1193 and, after years of study, became a bishop of the Roman Catholic Church.

It is said that he was one of the first men to dissect animals in order to find out how their bodies were put together. Along the way, he developed the idea that the

Left, *Albertus Magnus, one of the greatest alchemists.*
Right, *A seventeenth-century artist's idea of what a homunculus might look like. Note the ancient flask.*

emerald was a magic stone that could cure growths on the human body. Another belief that he held was that there was such an animal as the *basilisk.*

The mythical basilisk was supposed to be an animal version of the homunculus. That is, it was an artificially created being. There are many legends about what the basilisk looked like. One legend says that it was a cross between a rooster and a snake. Albertus believed that if you could find a basilisk, burn it up, and collect the ashes, you would have a substance that would keep spiders away. He also thought that with these ashes, silver could be turned into gold.

So Albertus was credited with the belief that since these ashes could turn a base substance into gold, the philosopher's stone and the basilisk were about the same thing. Writers of the time claimed that Albertus had found this magic substance and turned it over to his student, Thomas Aquinas. Aquinas is supposed to have destroyed it, claiming that it was the work of the devil.

Legend also has it that Albertus made a robot in the shape of a man and kept it as a servant. But it is said that Thomas Aquinas destroyed the robot too because it was in the habit of talking too much.

Both of these men, Albertus and Thomas, became saints of the Roman Catholic Church. Both were brilliant and devout, and both believed in the idea of the homunculus.

Paracelsus comes back into the story at this point. He was the next man of importance to search for the homunculus. In fact, he developed a formula for producing this little man.

First, a man's semen was to be put into an airtight jar. Then the jar was to be buried in horse manure for forty days, with a magnetic field placed around it. During this time, the homunculus would begin to live and move. At the end of the forty days, it would resemble a man, although it would be transparent.

At this point, it was to be fed with human blood and kept at body temperature for forty weeks. At the end of this time it would look like a perfect human child, but it would be much smaller.

We can't be sure that Paracelsus believed in his own formula. He ended the prescription with the comment, "It may be raised and educated like any other child until it grows older and is able to look after itself."

Later in history, a certain physician, Dr. Borel, reported to the French king Louis XIV that he had made a little man that gave off rays of light.

Another alchemist, Robert Fludd, claimed that he had made a homunculus in a bottle from human blood. It had all been a big surprise to him, however. He hadn't known what he had done until he heard crying noises coming out of the bottle.

Of course these homunculus stories are odd. Who can believe that alchemists could grow a little man in a bottle? On the other hand, think of all the teams of scientists who are working right now on ways to create life in a test tube. Think of all the teams of technicians who are trying to create spare parts for the human body.

The search for knowledge goes on. We want to acquire knowledge in order to learn about life, of course. But we also want to make this a better world for every human being. And this search for the understanding of life is what this book is all about.

A Matter of Life and Death

Where did life come from? How did it happen? One of the most popular scientific theories says that the earth is about 4.7 billion years old and living organisms appeared on it about 1.2 billion years later. The question is, what went on during those lifeless years that led to the emergence of living things?

Dr. Cyril Ponnamperuma has been studying this question for years. The Ceylon-born scientist has worked on the problem at the University of California at Berkeley, at the National Aeronautics and Space Administration's Ames Research Center in California, and at the University of Maryland's Laboratory of Chemical Evolution.

Ponnamperuma believes that life was inevitable on the earth because of the chemical makeup of the planet. But he also says that if we become capable of wiping ourselves out, and destroy ourselves along with every other living thing, life will never reappear here. The conditions favorable to the beginnings of life do not exist anymore on our planet.

As far as we know, this is probably the way in which life came about on the earth. First, the universe was made up of hydrogen gas. About 13 billion years ago, this gas exploded. The result was many whirling particles of heavier chemical elements.

About 4.7 billion years ago, the earth and the other planets congealed out of this chemical dust cloud. The earth's first atmosphere was made up of methane, ammonia, and water vapor.

For hundreds of millions of years, this atmosphere was being hit by ultraviolet light, X rays, and other radiation from the sun. Volcanos were created. Thunder and lightning were in the atmosphere. All of this energy began to change and reorganize the compounds in the atmosphere. The result was probably the creation of simple organic compounds necessary to life, such as amino acids.

There are other theories about how the earth came into being. One of them states that a passing star came too close to the sun, and its gravitational pull caused parts of the sun to fly off into space. These parts then became the planets. This star, of course, would be billions of light-years away by now.

Most scientists feel that it took a long time for life to appear on the earth. Ponnamperuma and others have carried out experiments in which they reproduced the earth's early atmosphere and bombarded it with one kind of energy or another. This produced, among other things, amino acids— the building blocks of protein molecules. And protein is one of the two vital compounds of living things.

For all living things on the earth have two basic molecules: the nucleic acids that make up the genes and control heredity, and the proteins that carry out the orders of the

Dr. Cyril Ponnamperuma with a meteorite in which he discovered amino acids, one of the main constituents of living cells. The question is, how did they get there?

genes. Everything that living things do as living things is the result of basic interactions between nucleic acids and proteins.

But what is a living thing? A simple answer might be that it is either an animal or a plant. And since both of these organisms are alive, they must share certain life processes. These are the things that all living creatures, plants and animals both large and small, must do in order to be called alive. There are ten of these life processes.

Number one is food getting. Basically, living things can get their food in two ways. Green plants make their own food by means of a process called photosynthesis. In this process, carbon dioxide and water are combined in the presence of chlorophyll and light energy to form simple sugar and give off oxygen as a waste product. So green plants are pretty close to being self-sufficient when it comes to getting food.

But everything else that is alive must depend upon other living things for food. Humans, for example, must eat either meat from other animals, vegetables from the plant kingdom, or products of these living things such as honey and milk. By the way, do you remember the biblical reference to the Land of Milk and Honey? That was a place where humans could get food without ever having to kill another living thing.

The second life process is digestion. Once the plant or animal gets its food, what does it do with it? Of course, we can bite into a candy bar, chew it up, and spit it out. But what good would that do, aside from helping us to avoid gaining weight?

No, the food must be digested. Let's take a hamburger for an example. Once it gets into the stomach, it cannot enter the body's cells in the form of little pieces of meat, little drops of catsup, and little crumbs of bun. Something has to happen to it first. That something is called digestion.

Digestion really begins in your mouth. While your teeth are chopping up the hamburger, an enzyme in your saliva is working on the starch in the bun. An enzyme is a chemical substance that controls chemical reactions in living matter. The enzyme produced by the salivary glands, called amylase, is changing some of the starch into maltose, a form of sugar.

When you swallow, your chewed-up hamburger eventually gets to the stomach, where some other things happen. Your stomach muscles are grinding up the food and some digestive juices are going to work. These digestive juices, containing other enzymes, are breaking the food down further, softening it and helping to lubricate it for its trip through the rest of the digestive tract.

In the stomach, gastric juice is contributing enzymes that change some proteins into other forms of protein. Pancreatic juice contains enzymes that change starch into maltose, fats into fatty acids and glycerine, and proteins into amino acids.

Then the remains go into the small intestine, where digestion is completed by the intestinal juice. Enzymes change sugars into simple sugars and proteins into amino acids. The waste products continue to the large intestine, but the food that is of value has been broken down so that the body can use it.

In green plants digestion is a bit simpler. It might

involve just the changing of starch into sugar. Food is stored in green plants in the form of starch. But it must be changed to sugar in order for the plant to use it as nourishment. Enzymes are needed to make this transformation. The point is that the food must be broken down into something that can get into the cells of the body of the living thing. So there is a difference between merely *getting* the food and *digesting* it.

Number three of the life processes is absorption. Now the food is in an appropriate state to get where it is needed. The molecules of the digested food are dissolved in water and are ready to be taken into the cells of the plant or the animal. They enter right through the outer covering of the cell itself. This is absorption.

Number four is respiration. Most living things take in oxygen from the air. The oxygen combines with the digested food in an oxidation, or burning, process. This releases the energy in the food in the form of heat. Of course there are waste products that come from this process. Water and carbon dioxide are two of them—but more of that later. The process of oxidation can be likened to the burning of a match. Energy is released in the form of light and heat. Waste products, water and carbon dioxide, are given off. And the ash remains.

So, the absorption process consists of taking in oxygen to burn up food and giving off water and carbon dioxide. Humans and many other animals do this by inhaling oxygen and exhaling waste products. Other living things may do this by taking in oxygen and giving off waste products through their body coverings.

There are a few living things, called anaerobic organisms, that can carry on respiration even when oxygen is not present. The bacterium that causes tetanus, or lockjaw, is an anaerobe. It can live inside a puncture wound after the flesh and skin have come together to seal off the injury. Inside the puncture, without oxygen, the bacterium can live and infect the body.

The fifth life process is assimilation. The food has been broken down, the energy has been released, but then what? Humans and other living things have food in their cells, mostly in the form of amino acids, water, fat, sugar, and minerals. But what good is it?

It can be turned into new protoplasm. Protoplasm is the living substance in the cells which is the basis for all life functions. In assimilation, the raw materials of protoplasm are organized into the stuff of life itself. So the process of assimilation may result in the growth of the cell or in the formation of new cells. And that will cause the growth of the whole organism. In humans it sometimes appears that growth stops after the age of twenty. But that is not completely true.

Cells do wear out. Think of the skin cells that are constantly wearing away, and don't forget those dandruff scales that can fall out of your hair. These cells need to be replaced, as do the blood cells that you lose when you cut yourself and the fingernail cells that you may bite off when you are nervous. And do not forget that you could never have gotten any taller than you were as a baby if you had not added new cells to your body.

Number six of the life processes is excretion. After

assimilation, there are still a lot of unwanted substances remaining. Living things get rid of their wastes through the process of excretion.

There are many kinds of organisms, such as the ameba and the paramecium, that have a body consisting of only one cell. Then there are other living things that have more than one cell but are still quite simple, such as the sponge. Both of these kinds of organisms have little trouble with the process of excretion. They live in water and just push the waste matter out through their cell coverings into the surrounding liquid. But larger animals and plants find it a little more difficult to excrete.

Each cell of the body of a more complicated animal must shove its waste out into the fluid that surrounds it. From there, the waste goes to the blood stream. Then the blood carries it to the kidney for liquid excretion, or the lung for gas excretion, or the skin for liquid excretion. Most leafy plants excrete gas and liquid wastes from their leaves at all times. Some plants also deposit solid wastes in their leaves and excretion is merely a matter of the dropping of the leaves in the fall.

The seventh life process is secretion. This is the way in which living things manufacture the chemicals they need to continue living. We have already mentioned some of the enzymes required for digestion; these are made by the organism. There are also lubricating liquids such as the mucus of the nose and digestive system. There are the hormones, chemical substances formed by special glands such as the thyroid, the pituitary, the ovaries, and the testes, that influence activities such as growth and reproduction. Insulin that regulates the digestion of carbohydrates, such as sugar, is also a hormone.

Number eight of the life processes is motion. All living things move. Of course, most of the motion in the plant kingdom is merely the movement of liquids inside cells.

But there are many living things that have the ability to move from one place to another by hopping, skipping, flying, swimming, etc. The motion involved in going from one place to another is known as locomotion. Some tiny organisms are covered with hairlike structures called cilia which wave back and forth in the water to move the living thing along. Other organisms have whips at the ends of their bodies. These whips are called flagella and they snap in the water, causing locomotion. Still other living things just ooze along, the cell and its contents simply flowing in one direction or another.

In the case of larger animals, it is the muscle tissue that does the job. These are the cells that move the arm or the leg, the wing or the tail, or any of the other body parts that carry the animal from place to place. And it is the muscle tissue that causes the internal movement of animals, too. The blood is pushed along by the heart muscle. The food is churned by the stomach muscles. And there are many more examples of the movement caused by muscle tissue.

The ninth life process is sensitivity, the capacity to respond to the environment. All living things react to their surroundings. Most plants bend their leaves toward light. Most exhibit root growth toward water. Some insects, such as the moth, fly toward the light; others, like the housefly, fly away from the light. Light, heat, sound, pressure, electricity, magnetism, and cold are just a few of the many factors to which most living things react.

Number ten of the life processes is reproduction. Without this process, there would be no living things after a few years. Even fleas must reproduce so that the flea population will not disappear from the face of the earth.

These are the ten things that a living thing must do in order to be called alive: get food, digest food, absorb food, take in oxygen, form new cells, give off waste products, manufacture the chemicals the organism needs, move, respond to its environment, and reproduce. A pretty fair definition of life might be that an organism is alive if it carries on all of these functions. But there is a middle ground to be considered.

For an example of this middle ground, we can look at the work of Dr. Robert J. White of Case Western Reserve University in Cleveland, Ohio. In 1964, he announced that he had been able to keep monkey brains alive for twenty-four hours.

These brains had been kept alive by circulating blood through the organs which give the brain oxygen and remove the carbon dioxide. All of this was done with a miniature heart-lung machine. But this machine could only take care of the oxygen and carbon dioxide levels of the blood. If the brains were to be kept alive any longer than about twenty-four hours, other waste products in the blood would have had to be removed. The Cleveland researchers could have done this by giving the brains a complete blood transfusion every three or four hours. But it was decided that this would be too expensive and time consuming, so the brains were allowed to die.

Then, in 1966, White and his colleagues reported that they had been successful in removing whole heads of dogs, cooling them to almost freezing for several hours, and then connecting them to the blood vessels of other animals. The blood vessels in the necks of the complete dogs kept the transplanted heads supplied with nourishment and removed the waste products.

Sometimes the brains of these dogs were kept alive for up to two days. Researchers knew the brains were alive because the transplanted heads showed signs of life. Their eyes reacted to light with pupil contraction, and their mouths opened and closed in gasps. So the individual nerve cells in the heads and brains must have been alive. One conclusion from this is that perhaps animal brains are not as fragile as we have always thought.

There are some other things to be considered here, however—that is, quite apart from deciding whether or not these heads and brains were really alive. In principle, these experiments may seem to be good things. Living organs were used in the laboratory so scientists could find out how they work. The organs were treated with new drugs, and the effects of the drugs were measured.

Certainly, the brain is an organ that gets diseases just as any other organ does. And the Cleveland scientists pointed out that they wanted to use the animal brains to try to learn more about strokes. They hoped to get more information to be used for the prevention and cure of such brain malfunctions in man.

On the other hand, think about this. If those brains were truly alive, we could suppose that they might have been conscious. They might even have retained emotions. Who knows what terror, pain, and torture they have gone through without being able to express their feelings. It certainly is something to think about.

Probably, these dog and monkey organs were in a state between life and death. We have already mentioned the life processes. And although it might appear easy to define the point at which a living thing stops living, it isn't. In other words, we should be able to define death, but we really can't.

No one can even define a slow, natural death. It may be a gradual poisoning of the body cells. We know that it is usually more difficult to grow cells in a culture medium when the cells are taken from an old organism than it is when they are taken from a young living thing.

We know several things about the deterioration of the human body as it grows older. The first thing to degenerate is the muscle system. That is, fatigue sets in earlier than it used to. Then the vital capacity starts to decline. This is the amount of air that can be breathed out completely after a deep breath. This is normally between an upper limit of 2,200 cc (cubic centimeters) and a lower limit of 900 cc.

The tidal volume decreases, too. This is the quantity of air breathed in or out in each respiratory cycle of inhaling and exhaling. The average human tidal volume is about 500 cc. Old people average about 370 cc, or a 25 percent reduction. The number of white blood cells is lowered, and the powers of seeing and hearing are reduced. But at what point all of this deterioration results in death, no one can say.

We can lose our capacity for performing one or more of the life processes, like movement or reproduction, and still be alive. We used to believe that when our hearts stopped, we were dead. But now we know that there are many people walking around whose hearts have stopped for a time, as we shall see later.

In 1965, Dr. Friedhelm Schneider of Tübingen, West Germany, pointed out how extremely hard it is to define death. As an example, he mentioned the one-celled organism, the ameba. This tiny living thing reproduces by dividing itself into two amebas. These two then divide to become four, then eight, then sixteen, and so on. All the resulting amebas are still alive. So no ameba has died in the process. Is the original ameba dead? Or can we say that it is almost immortal? Schneider observed that one of the main things necessary for a death certificate is a corpse. And there is rarely an ameba corpse to be found.

There is another definition of death that is inaccurate, Schneider said. We usually say that a living thing is dead when its body functions stop. Living things are dead if they do not eat, breathe, move, etc. But rats have had their body temperatures lowered to $-328°$ F (Fahrenheit) for a short time. And when they were unfrozen, they showed no ill effects. Their body functions, of course, had been completely stopped for a time, but they were brought back to normal. Were they dead and then brought back to life? Or is death more than the stoppage of body functions?

In May of 1974, two California scientists discovered creatures in Antarctica that had been living in a frozen state for a length of time somewhere between ten thousand and one million years. The organisms were bacteria unlike any ever identified before. When they were thawed out in a laboratory culture, some of them were even able to reproduce. Tardigrades, animals that are relatives of ticks and mites, have been found frozen and have then been revived. They had existed for more than one hundred years in ice, without water, oxygen, or much heat. Yet when they were warmed and moistened, they started to move around.

So what is death? We often read newspaper stories about people who were revived hours after they had supposedly died. In 1964, the Algerian minister of foreign affairs was shot through the head. He stopped breathing, his heart stopped beating, and his brain was irreversibly damaged. He was clinically dead. But his blood was artificially circulated, and his heart started beating again—he lived for another three weeks.

Here is another case in which the loss of heartbeat was not a very good indication of death. In 1962, a great Russian physicist, Lev Landau, was in a horrible automobile accident. His physicians kept him alive for four days, but then his heart stopped beating and his blood pressure registered zero. Was he dead?

Massive drug injections and blood transfusions were given to the man, and his heart started to beat again. During the next week his heart stopped three more times, but he was rescued each time. After sixty days in a coma, he was past the crisis. Landau lived, his brain functioning, for six more years after his ordeal.

There are also a lot of questions to be answered about the actual time of death. When did the patient actually die? How long should physicians maintain a patient who will never recover consciousness? Who will switch off the machines?

These are important questions, since we are now in the

age of surgical transplants. In 1967, the French Academy of Medicine decided that its definition of death should be re-worked. They said that the stoppage of brain functions could be used as a sign of death. Once death had been thus estab-lished, the functioning organs of the patient could be kept working by artificial means. So that a patient who was un-conscious and could not be brought back to the conscious state could be used as a *bank* for organs for transplants and grafts.

In 1968, the Council for the International Organization of Medical Science of the World Health Organization defined death. They described it as a combination of disasters. The person who is dead does not react to anything around him, such as loud noises, or have any reflexes, such as the blinking of the eye in strong light. Muscle tone is gone. Breathing stops. Blood pressure drops rapidly. An electroencephalo-gram, a reading of brain waves, indicates no activity.

That may sound fairly thorough, but sometimes, even when the brain-wave reading has been zero for twenty-four hours, the patient may not be dead. There was a case in Israel of a fifteen-year-old boy who had a flat electroen-cephalogram for two weeks and yet recovered.

In the United States, there has been a great deal of argument about when to consider a person dead. Some of the questions have arisen in court. A well-publicized case in California in 1973 involved a victim who had been shot in a fight. The man had been rushed to a hospital and hooked up to various life-supporting machines. His heart and lungs were working, but the doctors said that his brain was dead. So his heart was removed and used in a transplant operation.

The lawyers for the man who did the shooting maintained that their client was not guilty of murder. They claimed that the doctors who removed the heart had killed the victim. This excuse was not allowed in court, but the question still remains—at what time did the man die, and what was the cause of his death?

The state of California has set up a committee of physicians, clergymen, and lawyers to come up with a definition of death. The state of Kansas, in 1970, defined death as "an absence of spontaneous respiratory and cardiac function and ... attempts at resuscitation are considered hopeless." What this means, of course, is that the patient's breathing and heartbeat have stopped and the doctors cannot get him to come back to consciousness.

On the other hand, the state of Maryland, in 1972, defined death as "the absence of spontaneous brain function, if it appears that further attempts at resuscitation or supportive maintenance will not succeed." What this means is that a person is dead if his brain has stopped sending out signals and the doctors feel that they cannot bring him back to consciousness or even keep him alive.

The variation in legal definitions of death is shocking. We need a definition of death that everyone—especially doctors, clergymen, and lawyers—will accept. What a sorry situation it is when a person can be legally alive in Kansas, and at the same time be legally dead in Maryland—or vice versa.

Artificial Parts

It has been said that, in a way, all biological laboratory work tends toward the creation of life. Not that biologists have done this, of course, but they are seeking ways to better understand life in order to prolong and improve it. Cancer researchers are trying to find a cure for this disease. Agricultural researchers are trying to find a way to produce better food. Psychological researchers are trying to find ways to help us live well-adjusted lives.

And in a way, a great deal of technological laboratory work tends toward the creation of mechanical life—spare parts for the human body. No one could ever say that artificial parts can truly substitute for the real thing. But by creating them, technicians, like researchers, are seeking ways to prolong life and make it more enjoyable.

Artificial limbs are not new. They are pictured in ancient Egyptian and Roman drawings; they were replacements for arms and legs lost in battle. Peg legs go back as far as 600 B.C. In the Middle Ages, iron forearms, hands, and legs were common. Metal hands have been used for about four hundred years. Even Paul Revere made false teeth.

So, for the last few centuries, we have been using artificial parts for people. Everyone accepted Captain Hook's artificial hand and Long John Silver's artificial leg. No one was surprised at George Washington's false teeth. Until recently, however, most artificial human body parts were worn on the outside of the body and usually only during the day. How times have changed.

Now we might meet someone with an artificial leg or arm and not even be aware of it. And soon we may be able to create artificial appendages that are really undetectable. They may be artificial in the sense that they will be made in an engineering workshop and operated by mechanical muscles. Or they may be artificial in the sense that they might once have belonged to another human being. But for all practical purposes, they will be normal, functioning parts of the body.

For the time being, let's forget the types of prostheses that can be taken off—false teeth, eyeglasses, wooden legs, and so forth. Let's concentrate on those that are permanently attached to the human body. For years, we have been able to put metal plates in broken skulls. We have used plastic tubes as replacements for sections of arteries and veins. And we have regulated the heartbeat with pacemakers imbedded in a patient's body.

In the future, we will have to get over the idea that a person with an artificial heart is not as good as someone with a real heart. We must not assume that an artificial heart makes a person less human. This will be hard to do since many people regard the blind or crippled as handicapped for life. But are they permanently handicapped?

In 1935, a book was published called *The Circus of Dr. Lao.* In it, author Charles Finney described a lawyer named Frank Tull:

> His teeth had been fashioned for him and fitted to his jaws by a doctor of dental surgery. His eyes, weak and wretched, saw the world through bifocal lenses, so distorted that only through them could the distortion of Frank's own eyes perceive things aright. He had a silver plate in his skull to guard a hole from which a brain tumor had been removed. One of his legs was made of steel and fiber.... In his left arm a platinum wire took the place of the humerus.... On one ear was strapped an arrangement designed to make ordinary sounds more audible.... A wig covered the silver plate in his skull. His tonsils had been taken from him, and so had his appendix and his adenoids. ...Water had been drained from his knee.... He carried his head in a steel brace.... One hundred years after he died, they opened his coffin. All they found were strings and wires.

All of these artificial parts were in use when the book was written. But during the next thirty years, medical research came a long way. Let's take a look at how things stood in 1965, thirty years after the book was published.

Prior to this time, it had been possible to stop a patient's blood circulation for a time, but not long enough for a surgeon to perform the open-heart surgery necessary to repair a heart valve. The blood must circulate or the patient will die. But by the mid-sixties, a heart-lung machine had been developed. It acted as a substitute for the patient's heart and lungs during an operation, causing the blood to be circulated and furnished with oxygen. This machine enabled the surgeon to work on the heart, since it could now be emptied of blood.

One of the most spectacular developments in heart surgery was the invention of artificial spare parts. Sometimes parts of the heart and circulatory system are damaged beyond repair. When this happens, the only hope for the patient is a replacement part. By 1965, artificial valves and blood vessels made of plastic were being used to replace defective natural parts.

Also, at that time, at the University of Michigan, as many as 150 people were coming regularly to a clinic to have the texture of their blood checked. They had all been the victims of strokes and heart attacks caused by blood clots that blocked the blood vessels which supply the heart. When a blood clot develops inside a person's circulatory system it will travel along until it comes to a small opening or vessel, which it may then plug.

Some of the cells served by the plugged vessel may not receive nutriments or oxygen, in which case they will die. If this happens often enough in the more sensitive parts of the body, the patient will die or be seriously damaged. For example, if the brain cells are deprived of oxygen for just a few minutes, the patient may lose his reasoning abilities. The Michigan clinic was trying to prevent this by injecting drugs which reduce the blood's tendency to clot. This, in a sense, was the creation of an artificial blood part.

Another development completed by 1965 was the heart pacemaker. The heart beats in response to nerve impulses. Sometimes disease destroys the rhythm of these impulses or may even stop them. When this happens, the heart will sometimes stop. If it does not start again, the result, of course, is death.

The pacemaker was developed to help people with defective nerve impulses. It is an electrical device which sends pulses to the heart to keep it beating in rhythm. The pacemaker has saved countless lives, and its use has allowed people with this type of heart defect to lead almost normal lives.

To bring the story up to date, let's look at what has been going on since the mid-sixties. And let's begin with devices for the handicapped. In 1965, at the Case Institute of Technology in Cleveland, researchers were working on restoring motion to a paralyzed limb. They felt that if the trouble was in a faulty nerve and the muscles were still in good working order, something could be done.

A patient with paralyzed arms and legs was the subject of the experiment. And he was finally able to eat with his right hand. It worked like this. A device called a transistor stimulator was built and attached to the hand to permit the patient to clench his fist and pick up objects. The transistor stimulator was connected to electrodes placed in the skin near the shoulder muscle called the trapezius. When the brain sent electrochemical signals to the trapezius telling it to contract, the signals were picked up by the electrodes. The signals then bypassed the damaged nerve and went to the transistor stimulator. The hand clenched, and the patient was able to grab a spoon. Of course, this stimulator was far too expensive and bulky to be used by most handicapped people, but the research findings were extremely valuable.

A system also was developed to make possible five other types of motion. A patient was equipped with a pair of eyeglasses that had a small arc lamp in the frame. This is a lamp in which the light is caused by an electrical discharge between two electrodes—one of the most common types of arc lamp is the welder s arc. The patient could point the beams of the lamp toward one of a series of photoelectric cells on a table in front of him. Whichever one he selected would cause his arm to do something. It might twist the wrist or rotate the upper arm, for example. The patient could stop the movement by blinking his eyes. Once again—expensive and bulky, but a step in the right direction.

In Australia, in 1966, a surgical team corrected, with a titanium cable, a spinal curvature in a thirteen-year-old boy. The cable was surgically implanted in the boy's body on the curved side of the spine and tightened to a fifty-pound force of tension. This straightened out the spine and controlled the shape of the patient's back as he grew to adulthood.

The plastic and stainless-steel hip joint goes back to 1962. Between three and four million Americans have a certain kind of arthritis of the hip. It is caused by a breakdown of the cartilage in the hip joint. This joint is a ball-and-socket arrangement with cartilage between the two parts to aid in cushioning the shocks of movement.

But there is hope for repair. Thousands of people have been provided with plastic and metal substitutes for the joint. And the developer of this device received the Albert Lasker Clinical Medical Research Award in 1974.

Dr. John Charnley of Wrightington Hospital in Wigan, England, began his work in the mid-fifties. At that time, the common hip-joint repair operation was to cut off the ball end of the thighbone, then replace it with a stainless-steel ball shaped like the original. But with no cartilage left in the joint, too much dependence was placed on lubrication by body fluids. Some people's hips actually began to squeak. Charnley realized that soon friction in the joint would cause the stainless-steel part to work loose from the thighbone.

He chose Teflon to replace the stainless steel in the operation. Teflon is the plastic that is used to coat stainless-steel razor blades and greaseless frying pans. And it has the lowest friction rating of any known solid. He made both thighbone balls and hipbone sockets out of the plastic. But the Teflon wore out after about a year.

The next step was to try a high-density polyethylene that was more sturdy. He put this material to use in the hip socket and went back to stainless steel for the ball of the thighbone. The friction was low enough so that the body's natural fluids could lubricate the artificial joint. He used a new kind of acrylic plastic to hold the steel ball firmly in place on the thighbone. As of now, it is estimated that between fifteen and twenty-five thousand of these artificial joints are being implanted every year.

Today, metal alloys are being used to make knuckle joints for thumbs and fingers. Metal and plastic knees have been developed. Work is being done on artificial ankle and elbow joints. There has been some success with plastic and stainless-steel shoulder joints. All of these are being used to relieve victims of severe arthritis.

In 1968, a Russian team, L. S. Alejew and S. G. Bunimowitsch, developed a technique to aid certain types of handicapped people. These patients had damaged nerve connections between their brains and their arms or legs.

As mentioned before, nerve impulses are electrical and

travel along the nerves as a sort of current. Imagine that you want to pick up a pencil. Your eye sees the pencil and sends a message along a nerve to the brain. The brain sends a message along a nerve to the hand and fingers. The fingers put pressure on the pencil and a message goes back to the brain that the pencil has been picked up. If the nerves between the eye and the brain or the brain and the hand have been damaged, the pencil cannot be picked up. You might not see the pencil. Or your fingers might not be able to do what the brain tells them to do.

The Russian team amplified and stored on computer tape the electrical impulses that stimulated muscle movement in healthy people. These recorded electrical impulses were then used to produce similar movement in the limbs of patients with damaged nerves. The movements of the muscles of the arms or legs of these patients were stimulated electrically by bypassing the places where the nerves were not functioning. The patient or the doctor could ask for a certain movement to be reproduced. Then that part of the tape would be run. An electrical impulse would come from the machine through a wire attached to the arm or leg of the patient. And the limb would move.

This sounds like an ideal way to exercise a paralyzed limb. But there was more to it than that. There were occasions when a sort of learning process occurred, and healthy, nearby nerves gradually took over for the damaged nerve. In this way, normal movement was sometimes restored to the patient's limbs.

In 1974, Dr. Maurycy Silber, of the Bird S. Coler Hospital in New York, demonstrated a pneumatic orthesis.

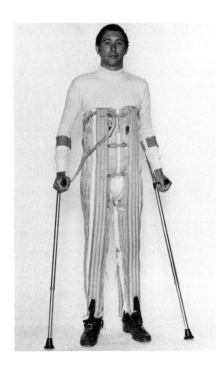

The pneumatic orthesis,
a possible replacement for
metal braces. Made of nylon,
this lightweight device gives
support to a paralyzed patient's
entire body.

A fourteen-year-old boy who had been burned at the age of two wore the device. His spinal cord had been permanently damaged, causing paralysis from his waist down. With the pneumatic orthesis, he was able to go up and down a flight of stairs with the aid of crutches.

Designed to replace conventional metal braces, the nylon garment weighs less than five pounds and can be worn under the patient's regular clothing. It is inflated to thirty-two pounds of air pressure per square inch, giving support all over the patient's body.

Manufactured by ILC Dover, of Dover, Delaware, the orthesis may eventually be used by millions in the United

States alone. In this country there are about 130,000 paraplegics (people paralyzed from the waist down), 2.5 million hemiplegics (people paralyzed on one side), 500,000 stroke victims each year, and many polio, muscular dystrophy, and cerebral palsy patients. It is too early to tell how many of these people can be helped by the pneumatic orthesis, but tests are going on in several parts of the United States to find out.

Victims of muscular sclerosis may be helped to walk and even drive automobiles by a neuropacemaker developed by Dr. Albert W. Cook of the Downstate Medical Center in Brooklyn, New York. Tiny electrodes are implanted in the spinal cord of the patient. These are hooked up to small radio receivers placed under the skin. The patient carries a battery-operated transmitter that sends electrical messages to the electrodes, bypassing the damaged nerves. This too is still in the experimental stage.

The myoelectric hand is an artificial device that moves by means of electrical signals. One of these devices was developed in England for the Medical Research Council by scientists at Hendon and St. Thomas Hospitals in London. Then the Atomic Weapons Research Laboratory in Aldermaston took the machine and made it look more like a normal hand. All the miniature circuits and drives were covered by a plastic glove that looks like a real human hand.

The hand is attached by a socket to the stub of a missing arm. And it has a small, direct current, electric motor which can move the first two fingers toward the thumb. This is done by signals from sensors that have been attached to the stump of the arm. The sensors pick up the nerve signals that come from the brain through the nerves of the arm muscle.

In the fingers of the hand are strain gauges that measure the amount of pressure being used and signal that information back to the sensors and thus to the brain. So the hand can pick up a glass tumbler without breaking it. These hands exert about eight pounds of pressure. This is enough for most gripping situations.

This is an example of how the electrical nature of the human body can be used to aid the handicapped, and work continues in this arena. But early in 1975, Dr. Dudley S. Childress of Northwestern University made a statement to the press. "Myoelectric control," he said, "has not been as revolutionary in prosthetics as originally hoped, the Six-Million-Dollar Man notwithstanding. Nevertheless, it can produce dramatic prosthetic results and it is benefitting thousands of amputees around the world." He also pointed out that its big advantage is that no control harness is needed. Also, the wearer learns to use a myoelectric limb unconsciously, almost like a person moves his own arm, hand, or leg.

In 1975, Dr. Pierre Rabischong of the National Institute of Health and Medical Research in Montpellier, France, told of a motorized pneumatic suit that the French are developing. The suit has four motors—two of them are used for the hips and two for the knees. His big problem, he confessed, was making the motors small enough so that the suit could be worn without discomfort by a paraplegic. Electric motors are heavy and make too much noise. Hydraulic devices are better, but they have the problems of oil leakage and lack of sufficient energy supply.

The comfort of a patient often depends upon the fit of the limb. Now, computers are being used in the fitting of artificial legs. At the Valenton Center of Re-education near Paris, France, patients wearing new artificial legs walk along a special track. The test floor is connected to the computer, and as the patient walks, the machine records the patient's weight, the patient's stride length, and the reaction of the limb upon contact with the floor. Before the computer was installed, it took the staff about six hours to test the results of the fitting of an artificial leg. With the computer, eight to ten separate fittings can be carried out in an hour. The machine tells how well the leg fits, without tiring the patient, and it allows the person to exercise the new leg.

Much work has also been done in aiding people whose sense organs are damaged. As long ago as 1962, scientists were taking a tip from the bats. Bats detect and avoid obstructions by bouncing very high-pitched squeaks off obstacles in their paths. Experiments have shown, for example, that the North American bat, *Myotis lucifugus,* can safely make its way through a room strung with wires the size of human hairs. Scientists used the winged mammal's ability to see in the dark as the basis for an instrument that allowed a blindfolded person to walk unerringly around objects.

Developed by electronic expert Alvin E. Brown of Lockheed, the device looked like a medium-sized black box. A person carrying the bat sonar instrument could maneuver in the dark around such obstacles as trees, filing cabinets, cars, and other people. He could walk toward a wall, locate an open door in it, and pass through the opening without seeing or touching the doorway.

The instrument worked in much the same way as the bat sonar. The person held the case in front of him. The case was equipped with a voice that emitted sounds too high for the human ear to hear. The sounds were projected directly in front of the patient.

The instrument's range was about twenty feet. If there was an obstacle in front of the subject, the sounds reflected from the object and were converted into electrical energy which was sent to the operator's earphones. The loudness of the earphone clicks told the wearer how far he was from an object. As he walked toward it, or it came toward him, the signal got louder. If there were no sound in the earphones, the patient knew that the way ahead was clear. Unfortunately, not much came of this device. It worked all right, but it was too cumbersome, since it required the patient to use both hands to carry the box. This might have been better than nothing, but the earphones blocked out any other sounds, so the patient's normal hearing was impaired.

Because of a device developed by L. Balmer, at the Lancaster College of Technology at Coventry, England, blind people may be able to participate in track meets. He built a three-pound detecting apparatus that was attached to a sightless runner. Then a wire was laid down on both sides of the running lane on the track.

A current was sent through the wires in the ground, setting up a magnetic field along the track lines. If you have ever made an electromagnet in school, you know that a magnetic field can be found around a current-carrying wire. The runner had strapped the detecting device around his waist. This machine picked up the magnetic field and changed the magnetic energy to sound signals. The sound, stereo signals, was carried to headphones that the runner wore.

As long as the runner stayed an equal distance between the lines, he heard the signals at equal volume in each ear. If the signal in one ear was weaker, he had to correct his position to stay in the center of the lane. In practice, the device worked. But it was expensive. The blind runner was carrying extra poundage that slowed him down. And he had to listen to the sounds and so lost part of the concentration necessary to run as fast as he could.

Most blind people see through their ears, fingertips, and noses. But scientific work that will help them to see artificially continues. In 1968, at Cambridge University in England, Drs. G. S. Brindley and W. S. Lewin implanted a sheet of electrodes beneath the skull of a blind woman. The electrodes were connected to her visual cortex, the outer layer of the eye. When electricity was sent through the electrodes, the patient reported a sensation of seeing light.

Brindley and Lewin found that when they varied the strength and frequency of the signals, the patient received light sensations at different points on the visual field. She was also able to tell the difference between signals from two different electrodes that were only one-tenth of an inch apart. The success of this experiment caused some scientists to think that if enough electrodes were connected, the patient might be able to read.

Professor Armando del Campo of the National University of Mexico has had some success, too. Using a combination of photosensitive agents that convert images into electrical signals, he has taught patients to see. That is, they can see well enough to avoid obstacles. They are also able to locate objects on a table.

At the present time, Dr. William Dawson, of the University of Florida, is working on a synthetic eye. His group of researchers is trying to develop a partially artificial retina. The retina is the innermost portion of the eye and it might be called the real seeing instrument. It is the part of the eye where the incoming light rays are focused and their impulses are sent on to the brain.

Dawson points out that retinal disease and damage cause about 20 percent of all blindness and are usually incurable. Corneas and lenses of the eye have already been made synthetically. If a partially artificial retina can be developed, many blind people will be able to see.

Dawson has placed a tiny electrode on the outer surface of the eye. This transmits a small electrical current to the inner layers and can cause a blind person to see light, as Brindley and Lewin found out. That is, if the current is focused on the undamaged portion of the retina.

So far, the human subjects have been able to see light only, not images. But if the light converters could be made to stimulate enough nerves, an image might be possible. Dawson has hopes for success by 1983.

A device has been built that lets blind-and-deaf people hear the doorbell. It is a hearing aid that can be worn on the finger like a ring. When the doorbell is rung, an impulse goes through an electrical circuit in the house. This, in turn, sets up a magnetic field inside the house. The magnetic field activates the pickup coil of the ring, and the vibrations can be felt by the user. However, this does seem like a complicated way to find out that someone is at the door.

In 1974, it was announced that a primitive, implanted hearing aid had been developed by Dr. William F. House of the Ear Research Institute in Los Angeles. It involves inserting platinum electrodes in the cochlea of the ear and connecting them to an induction coil inserted behind the ear. The auditory nerves are in the cochlea. This coil stimulates these nerves by picking up sound signals from a tiny transmitter attached to a type of eyeglass frame. Several patients have been helped by this device.

For some people who cannot speak, Dr. Stanley Taub of the New York Medical College has developed a small device. It aids those who have had their larynxes and vocal cords removed. The machine, a case containing a valve system, is worn on the chest. It regulates the flow of air from one opening on the side of the neck to another one that leads into the windpipe.

But on to the circulatory system. Synthetic fibers are now being used to replace blood vessels. This was first done in 1953 by Dr. Charles Hufnagel of Georgetown University in Washington, D.C. He used Orlon, but now knitted Dacron is more often used.

Artificial heart valves have been implanted in thousands of people. As of 1974, two surgeons, Dr. Michael E. DeBakey and Dr. Denton Cooley, had performed this operation more than seven thousand times.

In 1966, an artificial heart chamber was permanently implanted in a patient, a sixty-three-year-old woman. This operation was done by Dr. Adrian Kantrowitz, a surgeon at

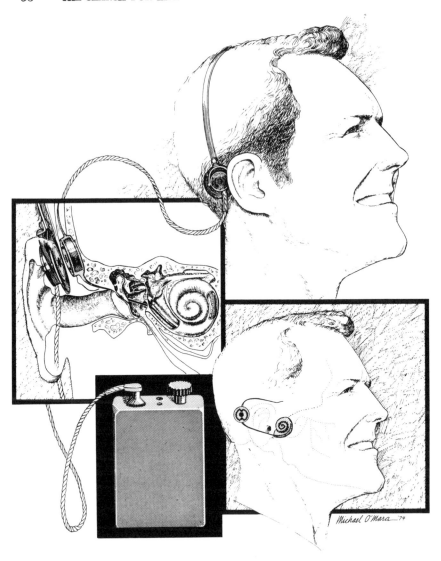

Top, *the transmitter for this implantable hearing aid can be worn like a headset.* Bottom right, *drawing shows where the electrodes and the induction coil are inserted;* center left, *the complete device.*

Maimonides Hospital in Brooklyn, New York. The artificial chamber had been developed by Dr. Kantrowitz and his brother, Dr. Arthur Kantrowitz, a physicist of Everett, Massachusetts.

The first attempt to replace the pumping action of the human heart with a machine was carried out with partial success in 1963. Dr. Michael DeBakey, professor of surgery at Baylor University's Medical School in Texas, used a plastic heart pump on a forty-two-year-old man undergoing surgery to repair his aortic valve. This is the valve that controls the flow of blood from the heart's main pumping chamber, the left ventricle, into the circulatory system.

Though the valve was repaired successfully, the surgeons realized that the patient's heart was not pumping strongly enough. They used an air compressor to take over the function of the left ventricle. A plastic tube was sewn into the patient, connecting the upper left chamber of the heart with the main artery that carries the blood. The compressor was connected to the plastic tube so pulsations of air could force blood into the artery without any help from the heart.

Although this particular patient lived only four more days, it was theoretically possible to keep a patient alive for weeks until his heart repaired itself and was able to take over the normal pumping action. Today, scientists are working on artificial heart pumps that could be inserted into the body and be powered by the patient's own muscles.

One of the mysteries about the circulatory system is the almost unfailing regularity of the heartbeat. The heartbeat is triggered by a nerve center in the heart wall. However, this mechanism sometimes breaks down. When it does, the necessary stimulation can often be provided by a pacemaker, or heart-starter.

In 1974, it was estimated that from fifty thousand to sixty thousand people had been supplied with pacemakers. And twenty-five thousand new pacemakers were being implanted every year. In January of 1975, a pacemaker was implanted in a two-day-old California baby.

The simplest kind of pacemaker is powered by a tiny, mercury, long-life battery implanted under the muscles of the stomach. There is a wire under the skin through which the pacemaker delivers a tiny shock to the heart sixty times per minute. This causes the heart to beat. The number of shocks per minute can be increased or decreased to meet the varied demands of the body. For example, the body would require more shocks when exercising than when sleeping.

One of the problems with the pacemaker, however, is that it requires a battery change about every two years. And this means a trip to the surgeon every twenty-four months. Then, a nuclear-powered pacemaker was developed. The power comes from a tiny grain of radioactive plutonium 238 imbedded in the center of the device and implanted in the patient's body. The radiation from the plutonium 238 creates heat that is converted to an electric current by a tiny, thermoelectric converter. Wires carry the electric energy to the electrodes imbedded in the heart wall, and the heart is stimulated to beat. The nuclear-powered pacemaker is expected to last up to ten years without a replacement.

In 1974, General Electric announced that it might soon be possible to have a sodium bromine battery for heart pace-

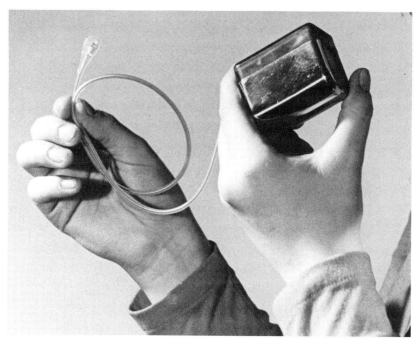

A nuclear-powered heart pacemaker, developed for the Atomic Energy Commission by ARCO Nuclear Company.

The battery (on the left) *for this implantable heart pacemaker* (shown actual size on the right) *can be recharged from an external power source.*

makers that could last more than ten years. It would be only half the size and one-quarter the weight of the common mercury zinc cells in use at that time. General Electric hopes to have its new battery in production by 1976.

Another kind of machine being perfected to help the human body has to do with the kidneys. The kidneys perform the task of removing poisonous waste products from the blood. All of the blood in the human body passes through the kidneys every three minutes. But when the kidney filters fail, their owner dies, unless he can get help. In the 1950s, an artificial kidney machine was developed, based on an earlier model designed by Willem Kolff. It could carry on the filtering process of the kidneys, called dialysis, outside the body.

Two or three times a week, the patient with defective kidneys must go to the hospital for treatment. His blood is circulated through the dialysis machine, and after it is cleansed, it returns to the body in a continuous round of circulation. But it is a wearisome process, and there is no practical artificial kidney in sight at this time. The patients must continue returning to the hospital for this expensive treatment.

Many of these kidney patients become very discouraged after a time. The expense, the discomfort, and the deadly dull routine—no vacations are possible—eventually exhaust them. Their depressed feelings and behavior apparently affect the people who look after them, too.

In 1968, a startling report came from Drs. A. Kaplan De-Nour and J. W. Czaczkes of the Hadassah University Hospital in Jerusalem. They were a part of a team that cared for patients who were being treated with kidney dialysis machines. Their study concerned the attitudes of the people on their team.

The physicians had feelings of guilt, probably because they were part of a system that decided who would live and who would die—there were just not enough kidney machines to go around. The doctors tended, as time went on, to avoid visiting the patients—a kind of withdrawal symptom—by inventing lame excuses.

The nurses were different. They suffered from feelings of possessiveness and overprotectiveness. They even conveniently forgot to give messages from the doctors to the patients. The nurses and the technicians would sometimes quarrel about who was the most important to the patient. It was almost like a television family. The nurses were the overprotective mothers, the doctors were the demanding fathers, and the patients were the children.

Worse news was to come. Early in 1974, a report was published that pointed out some risks in kidney dialysis care. It was found that in the cases of those who had been receiving artificial dialysis care over a long period of time, there was an increase in the rate of hardening of the arteries (atherosclerosis) and heart disease. But the risk of heart problems is worth it. There are over ten thousand people in the United States on dialysis. Without the kidney treatment, these people would not have lived long enough to have developed the circulatory defects.

But what about the brain pacemakers? Electrical stimulation of the brain has been experimented with for years. And research work on brain pacemakers has been going on for more than twenty years. Stimulators are placed within the skull and can be connected with specific parts of the brain in two ways. The method used depends on what is wanted from the pacemaker. Is chemical stimulation needed, or is electrical stimulation desired?

If chemical stimulation is needed, small tubes called cannulas are connected between the skull and the place where the chemical is needed in the brain. If electrical stimulation is required, the stimulator is placed within that part of the brain where it is needed.

Let's look at an example of chemical stimulation. The usual treatment for Parkinson's disease is a chemical called L–DOPA. This drug can cause dangerous side effects that sometimes make its use impossible. But if the drug can be delivered to the place in the brain where it is needed, it will not affect the rest of the body as much. So a cannula is placed at that point, extending back to the skull. On top of the skull, under the skin, is attached a tiny, electrical impulse pump holding a reservoir of the drug. Electrical contacts are attached to the pump. When the drug is needed, the pump can be activated.

Pacemakers have also proved useful for electrical stimulation. Paralyzed arms and legs of monkeys have been linked to computers and back to the brains of the animals. Some of the results have been interesting. When the monkey is presented with food, for example, its brain sends an impulse to the electrode in its brain. The message is fed to the computer and back to the arm nerves, bypassing the damaged nerves that have caused the paralysis. The hand then picks up the food.

Another kind of brain pacemaker has been developed

by Dr. Irving S. Cooper of St. Barnabas Hospital for Chronic Diseases in New York. He has implanted his stimulator in more than fifty patients. Electrodes are placed over the front and rear of the cerebellum of the brain. This is the brain part that has control over the movement of the muscles. Wires from the electrodes are run under the skin, down the neck, to the chest. There, two receivers are implanted. Taped over this spot is a miniature, battery-powered transmitter that sends tiny currents through the cerebellum.

Dr. Cooper says that this can stop "the disabling procedures of previously intractable epilepsy, reduce the spasticity of cerebral palsy victims, and ease the spastic paralysis that often follows a stroke." In short, it helps the cerebellum to control muscle movements.

Finally, scientists have been trying to create substances that the human body normally manufactures. In 1966, it was announced that a group of Chinese scientists had been successful in synthesizing crystalline insulin. This was the first time that a natural protein had been produced in a laboratory.

In that same year, E. Hayek of Innsbruck, Austria, reported some success in synthesizing bone material. His substitute was tested and was found to be very similar to natural bone, except that it lacked a few elements, such as sodium and magnesium, that are found in natural bone.

Now the Japanese have taken the lead in the development of artificial bones. Dr. Yasuto Itami has been successful in implanting a titanium and polyethylene thighbone. Other scientists have used woven Dacron cords to replace weakened or damaged tendons and to repair separated shoulders.

So the search to find artificial parts goes on. All over the world, scientists and technicians are looking for ways to repair the human body by inserting artificial parts or hooking the body up to machines. But what about using real parts to do the job? What about transplanting real organs into the body? For this is another area of research rich with possibilities for human health.

Transplants

The chances are that we will never see an advertisement like this for a heart transplant:

> AMAZING PUMP BARGAIN! Self-containing four-chamber pump, weighs only 300–350 grams, yet operates continuously for periods up to one hundred years or more. Ultra-sensitive computerized control varies output according to environmental conditions. Pump works equally well upside down, under water, at zero gravity or at ten times the force of gravity. As used in American and Russian space missions.

Spare-part surgery will probably never come to this.

When we talk about spare-part surgery, we may be talking about things that are given by a donor, such as kidneys, or corneas from eyes. On the other hand, we may be talking about synthetic things, such as plastic tubing and valves used in heart operations. But plastic tubing and valves do not replace whole tissues, such as skin, bones, and blood.

So let's stick to grafting. This is the transference of live cells from one place to another where they will have a chance of surviving. There are three main types of grafts.

Autografts are masses of tissues transferred from one place to another on the same individual. A common autograft is the skin graft. *Homografts* are tissues transferred from one individual to another of the same species. Corneal grafts and kidney transplants come under this heading. *Heterografts* are tissues transferred from one individual to another of a different species.

A good example of a heterograft occurred in November of 1963. A twelve-man surgical team at Tulane University Hospital performed a history-making operation. They transplanted the kidneys of a male chimpanzee to a forty-four-year-old man suffering from chronic kidney disease. The patient was kept alive for two months following the operation, which was itself considered successful. He died, finally, of pneumonia, rather than from any dysfunction of his transplanted kidneys.

The problem with the heterograft is that it is often rejected by the body. Anti-rejection drugs must be given to the patient to help his body accept the foreign organ. In the case of the man at Tulane Hospital, he had been treated with many kinds of anti-rejection drugs for seven days before the transplant operation. These drugs, which aided his body in accepting the kidneys, may have lowered his resistance to infection. Even though he lived for two months with functioning transplanted kidneys, the operation was not entirely successful because of incomplete control of his body's natural rejection mechanisms.

The body has an efficient way of distinguishing between protein—that is, flesh, or blood, or bone—that belongs to it and protein that does not. It recognizes cells that have genes like its own and accepts them. When cells from an individual with a different set of genes are introduced into the body, the body of the receiver may destroy the new cells. Antibodies form in the body of the receiver and attack the foreign protein, and the intruder is rejected. In a way, this is good. Without this mechanism, much of our protection against microorganisms such as bacteria and viruses would collapse.

A good example of how this works is the blood transfusion. Let's backtrack for a minute.

Blood transfusions—transplants of a kind, although most of us don't think of them that way—are not new. There is an ancient Greek legend that old King Pelias was made young again by means of a blood transfusion. The ancient Egyptians believed that transfusions could restore the soul. Apparently something like the modern transfusion began to become prominent about three hundred years ago, when European physicians transfused lamb and calf blood into human beings. At that time, they did it in ways that strike us as a little different from modern techniques. The animal was strung up, and its blood supply was attached by a hose to a blood vessel in the arm of the human. Then the doctors opened a blood vessel in the other arm of the person receiving the blood. They did this because they believed that human blood had to flow out to make room for the animal blood.

One well-recorded transfusion was done in England by two doctors, Richard Lower and Edmund King, in the seventeenth century. They transferred sheep's blood into Arthur Coga, a minister in Cambridge, England. This was reported by Samuel Pepys, the British writer, who commented, "He finds himself much better since, and is a new man, but he is cracked a little in the head."

Blood transfusions have come a long way since that incident; nowadays, most are successful. Responsible physicians no longer transfuse animal blood into human beings. And we have found out how to type blood. In one system of typing, most blood falls into categories known as A, B, AB, and O. The blood of the patient and the blood of the donor are matched by type before a tranfusion takes place. And we have found out a great deal about the kinds of blood that will cause antibodies to build up in the receiver.

Let's take an example of what happens when alien protein is introduced into the body. And remember that this is highly simplified.

There are different types of blood. If an incorrect blood transfusion is made, if the blood of the donor is not matched to the blood type of the patient, the patient's body immediately starts manufacturing antibodies. The antibodies will destroy the red blood corpuscles in the donor's blood. The donor's blood may be considered an antigen, that is, an unwelcome substance that causes the production of antibodies in the body of the receiver. In the case of blood, the antibodies cause the corpuscles to stick together in clusters. They are not able to flow, and eventually, they will be destroyed. In a sense, the receiver is destroying his own blood transfusion.

The same mechanism which causes the destruction of unwanted blood cells will go into action if any foreign tissue is introduced into a person's body. That tissue might be skin, or an organ like a heart or kidney, or a piece of bone.

When it comes to autografts, there is no problem of rejection. Taking a tissue from one part of the body and putting it into another part does not usually cause antibodies to be produced. This is because the genes in our cells are the same in all parts of the body. The genetic makeup matches.

On the other hand, homografts, the transfer of tissue from one person to another, may cause antibodies to be produced unless the donor and the recipient are similar in their gentic makeup. This is why identical twins are ideal donors for each other.

To understand that, we have to look at how twins come about. Although there are several ways, the two most common are identical twinning and fraternal twinning.

Fraternal twins may be no more alike than ordinary brothers and sisters. It may be that the only thing they have in common is the same birthday. About one birth in eighty is a twin birth. And three-quarters of the twin births are fraternal twins.

Twins are born when, by some accident, the female produces two eggs capable of being fertilized at the same time. Of course, two sperm are necessary for this to happen.

No two eggs from a mother have exactly the same assortment of genes. And the same can be said for the sperm of the father. Fraternal twins, therefore, may each have an almost completely different collection of genes. They may inherit entirely different characteristics, just as any two children in the same family do. One may be intelligent, the other stupid. One may be tall, the other short. One may be a girl, the other a boy.

On the other hand, identical twins come about quite differently. They are the result of the fertilization of a single egg by a single sperm. During development, the fertilized egg divides in two in such a way that two separate embryos are formed and two children are produced. Keep in mind that both children are the result of one original sperm and one original egg, so they have the same genes in their bodies. Naturally, they are also the same sex. Since they are genetically identical, it is likely that a homograft would be successful. A twin then, can frequently donate an organ to an identical twin; the chances that the transplant will be successful are high.

The oldest type of transplant is that of the cornea, the transparent membrane in the front of the eye. When the cornea is diseased or damaged, sight is lost. The first successful corneal transplant was performed in 1905. The patient had been burned in both eyes, and the donor of the cornea was a young boy whose eye had been removed because of a foreign body lodged in it.

The operation became common when a Russian scientist discovered that corneas from dead bodies could be used if the corneas were fresh enough. He also discovered that spare corneas could be stored at low temperatures in an eye bank. And the reason that corneal transplants are more successful than almost any other kind of transplant is that the cornea has no blood supply. Therefore, no antibodies come in contact with it.

Transplants   73

But perhaps this type of homograft will become less common. In 1968, Dr. José Barraquer, of Bogotá, Colombia, announced a new technique for improving eyesight. He had performed an operation more than one hundred times. It consisted of taking out the patient's cornea, reshaping and grafting a piece of a dead person's cornea onto it, and then replacing it. Some of the subjects were able to see quite well after the operation, even without eyeglasses.

By the 1940s, the grafting of human arteries had become a fairly common practice. These were homografts, and again, they were successful because arteries do not require a direct supply of blood. They are only conductors. Eventually, it was discovered that nylon or Teflon vessels could be used instead of arteries from dead bodies. Today, this is standard practice.

The kidney was the next subject for grafting. The first successful kidney transplant, in the late 1940s, was between identical twins. They had, of course, the same genetic background, so the new kidney was not rejected by the recipient. Since that time, kidney transplants between persons who are not identical twins, or between persons of similar but not identical genetic makeup, have taken place with limited success. But the rejection processes of the body still present a barrier to be overcome.

Bone autografts are almost always successful. After all, they come from the same body. But there are problems with these, too. So much material must be taken from one bone to use in another that the donor bone is weakened. Also, two incisions must be made—one at the point of repair, and one at the point at which the new material is gathered.

It is desirable, then, to find some means of bone repair

other than the autograft. The problem is not as difficult as it might seem. To begin with, bone tissue has relatively few cells and a lot of hard, calcified material that is really inter-cellular matter—a kind of filler. This means that animal bones can be used to repair human bones if the problem of rejection of those few protein molecules can be overcome.

Suppose that bone could be treated in such a way that only the mineral salts that give it its hardness remained. This material would have no protein and so would not cause the production of antibodies in the body of the patient. Such bone would not be rejected.

A method of producing this kind of bone, called anor-ganic bone, was developed in 1954 by Williams and Irvine at the Massachusetts Institute of Technology. Ivor R. H. Kramer, H. C. Killey, and H. C. Wright, three English scien-tists, have been able to make cattle bones anorganic and use them to repair bone tissues in sheep and rabbits. Perhaps the repair of human bones is next.

Heart transplants have become so nearly commonplace that people forget the astonished reaction of the public to the first such operation.

On December 3, 1967, Dr. Christiaan Barnard, a South African surgeon, performed the world's first human heart transplant. He and his team had been successful in human kidney transplants, and Barnard himself had successfully per-formed heart transplants on dogs.

The patient, Louis Washkansky, was about to die from a severely diseased heart. He agreed to be the patient. Find-ing the donor was more difficult. The donor had to be someone who had died shortly before the operation and was as genetically similar to Washkansky as possible, in order to cut down on the risk of rejection.

Then a young woman was brought to the hospital. She had been struck by a car and had died of a brain injury. Although dead, with no brain activity, her heart was kept beating and her breathing was continued by machines brought in to do the jobs. Her heart was in good condition and her blood and other tissues were a good match to Washkansky's.

Washkansky was ready. But then there was a delay. When the heart machine connected to the donor was shut off, her heart continued to beat. Barnard refused to remove the heart until it had stopped beating. After fifteen minutes of waiting, the heartbeat ceased. The donor's chest cavity was opened and her heart was removed. The organ was rushed to the operating room, where Washkansky waited, and was transplanted into his body.

During the operation, Washkansky's circulatory system had been connected to a machine. Now doctors stopped the machine, but the new heart did not beat. They turned on the machine, reestablished the flow of Washkansky's blood, then stopped the machine again. And the new heart still did not beat. Once more they tried it, and this time the transplanted heart began to beat.

Louis Washkansky lived for only eighteen months after the operation. He died of pneumonia, but his new heart had worked.

A heart transplant is an amazingly complicated operation. The receiver's circulation has to be kept going with a pump; at one point in the operation, he has no heart to do

The heart-lung machine in use during an operation.
Left, *the plastic tubing in which the oxygen bubbles are filtered out;*
bottom right, *the pump;* top right, *the motor.*

the pumping job. The connections with the new heart have
to be properly made. There are nerves and blood vessels
that have to be matched up. And there is the immune reaction to suppress. Otherwise the patient may die of an
infection, such as pneumonia. Let's take a closer look at
rejection and immunization.

The rejection problem was first noticed by a Nobelprize-winning scientist, the Russian, Elie Metchnikoff. About the turn of the twentieth century he wrote, "One day when the whole family had gone to a circus. . . . I remained alone with my microscope, observing the life of the mobile cells of a transparent starfish larva, when a new thought suddenly flashed across my brain. It struck me that similar cells might serve in the defense of the organism against intruders. . . . I fetched a few rose thorns and introduced them at once under the skin of some beautiful starfish larvae as transparent as water. . . . Very early the next morning I ascertained that it had fully succeeded."

The thorns had been destroyed. Metchnikoff reasoned that the lymphocytes, or white blood cells, in people were similar to the starfish's mobile cells. He believed that the lymphocytes, which he called phagocytes, protect the body. They do this by destroying and engulfing harmful bacteria and other foreign matter.

In the 1940s, Sir Peter Brian Medawar, director of the National Institute for Medical Research in London, went a step further. He said that the rejection of homografts was the result of an immune reaction. Later it was found that lymphocytes destroy any foreign protein material in the body whether it is a harmful virus or a transplanted organ. So, if the lymphocytes could be put out of action for a time, transplanted organs might be accepted by the receiver's body.

Out of all this came the discovery of antilymphocytic serum, or ALS. It is also called antilymphocytic globulin, or ALG. To put it simply, ALS slows down the activity of the lymphocytes. They cannot even produce antibodies.

It was prepared this way. Lymphocytes from the human

thymus gland, lymph nodes, and spleen were injected into horses. The horses, of course, developed antibodies against them. Serum extracted from the horses was purified into a concentrate that was rich in antibodies that would operate against human lymphocytes.

When the serum, or more properly, the antiserum, is injected into a patient before and after a transplant, the antibodies attack the lymphocytes. For the time being, the patient has no immune reaction that will reject the transplant. So the transplant has a chance of being successful.

Medawar and his colleagues found that homografts lived on even after the ALS treatment was stopped. The lymphocytes seem to remain inactive even after no horses' antibodies remain in the body. And ALS does not appear to create lasting side effects.

But ALS has to be used carefully. Too little and the body will reject the graft. Too much and the body will be vulnerable to other infections. The wrong dosage has been found to cause damage to the liver or even to cause the formation of antibodies that can attack the ALS itself.

But the transplants continue. By the end of 1968, 100 heart transplants had been performed. In the next six years, 241 had been done. But only 36 of those heart transplant patients were still alive in late 1974. Eight of them had survived for five years and one for six.

One of the most startling heart transplants occurred in November of 1974. Dr. Christiaan Barnard of the Groote Schuur Hospital in Cape Town, South Africa, had been the first surgeon to perform a heart transplant, you remember. But this time he was the first to perform a twin-heart operation, in which the patient was given a second heart to aid his own.

Ivan Taylor, a fifty-eight-year-old factory worker, was dying of heart disease. His heart attack had damaged the main pumping chamber of the heart, but the rest of the heart was normal. Barnard decided not to remove the heart, but rather to use the heart of a ten-year-old girl who had been killed in an auto accident as a backup for the patient's own heart.

The surgeon trimmed away the damaged tissue. Then the new heart was joined to the old in such a way that blood would enter the old heart, be pumped to the new, and then be pumped through the body.

On April 11, 1975—four months after the operation— Ivan Taylor died of a blood clot in the lung. Another patient had been given a second heart on New Year's Eve, and this man has been released from the hospital and is doing well.

All of the early transplants represented new and sometimes startling developments, and there was much excitement and little public outcry about them. Perhaps the lack of criticism had to do with the fact that no harm was seen as coming to the donors. In the case of blood transfusions, donors quickly replace the loss and are as good as new. Corneal transplants do not present an ethical problem, since the cornea is a type of tissue that remains healthy long after the rest of the body is quite dead. Finally, the kidney donor can give up one organ, retain the other, and still live a normal life.

With the advent of the heart transplant in the late sixties, public attitudes began to change. By that time, livers and pancreases had also been transplanted, and there was growing recognition that there were more than technical and medical hazards connected with these operations. There were ethical and social problems as well.

To begin with, there is a shortage of parts—even eye corneas. In 1974, a Columbia University professor, Amitai Etzioni, pointed out that it may someday be possible to enlarge the spare-parts bank by *farming* a human body after death. The body could be maintained in such a way that it would continue to produce blood and could be tapped for transfusions every other day. It could also be used as a source of skin grafts and liver, kidney, heart, lung, and other organ transplants. And it would serve as a culture medium.

This may sound like a possible solution to the shortage problem, but Etzioni questioned the ethics of the whole thing. He also pointed out that farming is different from removing a single organ, after the death of the patient, for use in transplantation. In farming, the body would be completely dismembered. In transplants, most of the body is buried in a normal manner. The sociology professor said, "My point in bringing it up is to caution against shoving the issue under the rug. It is a real possibility that should be dealt with at conferences involving humanists, legislators, and others."

And there is still the problem of trying to determine the moment of death of the donor so that the heart or kidneys or other organ to be used for transplanting can be removed. Death used to be easy to define. But now, with the advances of modern medicine, a person who has stopped breathing or whose heart has stopped beating can be kept alive for long periods of time.

What about this case? In 1965, scientists at the University of Amsterdam were able to keep a human heart alive and beating outside the body for six hours. Dr. Kirk Durer and his co-workers removed the heart of a seventy-year-old man one hour and a half after he had supposedly died of a heart attack. They placed the heart in a machine that supplied it with oxygenated blood, and the heart began to beat again.

The scientists said that their research was designed to find a way of starting a heart that had stopped during an operation. But it is possible that this heart could have been restarted while it was still inside the owner's body. This is just one example of the many ethical questions that arise in this type of research.

We also need to solve the problem of strange side effects that sometimes occur after transplants. For example, people who have been given a new kidney occasionally develop a condition known as transparent lung. Apparently, antibodies formed in an attempt to reject the kidney also attack the lung. The result is a high fever and interference with the process of getting oxygen from the lung into the bloodstream.

Kidney transplant patients also exhibit a higher incidence of cancer than normal. And heart transplant patients have an increased chance of having a stroke. Some people undergo a psychological change after their operations. They may feel excessively grateful or guilty.

Finally, we must face up to the fact that, when all is said and done, all of these medical developments involve experimentation with human beings. There are some questions to be answered.

Does the human guinea pig have the right to oppose

research that might benefit society, especially when the research may not directly help that individual?

When the patient gives what is known as informed consent, that is, when the chances of survival are fully explained, is that patient being told about all of the potential aftereffects of the operation? Do the scientists really know what might happen?

Must we continue trying to ensure that future generations be provided with a healthy and disease-free world? Or will this just result in overpopulation at the expense of the people who are now undergoing human experimentation?

We must come up with some answers.

5

Freezing

For decades, scientists and science-fiction writers have been thinking about freezing as a way of prolonging life. Perhaps we should say for centuries, for in 1745, René-Antoine de Réaumur was able to prolong the life of an insect chrysalis by refrigeration. This gave him the idea that it might be possible to do the same for humans.

Ever since the first person looked into the future of space travel, it has been known that an astronaut would have to live a lot longer than is usual in order to reach a planet outside our solar system. The flight might take hundreds of years. The obvious answer is to deep-freeze the spaceman and thaw him out when he arrives at his destination. The traveler would need very little food, if any were needed at all. And he would not age much during the long voyage.

But cryobiologists, scientists who study low-temperature biology, do not have much hope for this at the present time. In the early 1960s, two cryobiologists, G. F. Doebbler and C. W. Cowley, summed up their feelings: "We can reasonably well handle single cells, non-viable biological materials, and a few more complicated situations. Some insect larvae and some human tissues can be preserved in a viable state by present methodology. Even some whole animals can be *partially* frozen and revived."

They were referring to experiments with a galago, which is a small mammal. The galago had died while it was being cooled to 23° F. Its heart had stopped, as had its breathing. Then it was revived. But it really did die a day later when it developed a lung problem. At the time of this experiment, hamsters had already been frozen until 40 percent of their body water had turned to ice, and then they had been revived.

Doebbler and Cowley went on: "Freezing a complex multicellular higher animal may turn out to be as unreasonable as a search for a perpetual motion machine. Perhaps, in the final analysis, we shall find that all approaches to man's dream of 'suspended animation' lead not to this but rather to a more profound understanding of the basis of life and death."

The problem in freezing large animals like human beings is one of time. It is relatively easy to freeze the outer layers of the body, but it takes time for the cold to penetrate through to the center of the body. And we all know that when tissues are frozen too slowly, as in the case of frozen meat, their cells break down and the protoplasm flows out through the damaged outer membranes. This indicates that some cells are dead, and the animal cannot then be revived after freezing.

It has been found that freezing over a period of from one to two hours at a temperature of from –13° F to –49° F is about right. But when the outer layers of the body of a large animal have been subjected to those temperatures and have been frozen, the inner layers may not yet have been frozen. If you freeze the body long enough for the inner layers to remain frozen for one or two hours, the outer layers may suffer from freezer burn.

Something may come from the work of P. Mazur and his co-workers at the University of Tennessee-Oak Ridge Graduate School of Biomedical Sciences. Working with mice, they discovered that rapid cooling of embryos can kill. But if the embryo was cooled slowly, at about twelve degrees per hour, to −94° F, it could then be cooled rapidly to −320.8° F and have a good chance of survival.

Despite the difficulties involved, the research goes on. There are those who believe that the freezing of humans for long spaceflights is not the only reason for carrying on this research. In 1964, R. C. W. Ettinger wrote, "Popular articles on suspended animation have mentioned chiefly its possible use by astronauts on long interstellar voyages. This aspect is trivial. Its importance lies not in travel to the stars, for the few, but in travel to the future, for the many."

Ettinger suggested freezing the recently dead, the sick, and the aged. They would be stored until medical science had discovered a cure for their illness or aging. Then they would be thawed out and treated. However, Ettinger admitted that we do not yet have a sure way of thawing out these bodies without injuring them.

This idea is not new. Benjamin Franklin noticed that flies appeared to drown in wine but could be revived when they were put in the sunlight. He may not have been serious, but he wrote in a letter to a friend when he was in his sixties:

> Having a very ardent desire to see and observe the state of America a hundred years hence, I should prefer to any ordinary death the being immersed in a cask of Madeira wine with a few friends til that time, to be then recalled to life by the solar warmth of my dear country.

The idea of deep-freezing people until science can bring a body back to life has interested many people. Groups have been formed to set up cryogenic burial grounds. The Cryonics Society of New York, for example, had four persons frozen in its banks in the early 1970s.

But in 1974, there was a report on the state of cryogenic freezing of human corpses. Robert Nelson, the president of the California Cryonics Society, revealed that people seemed to be losing interest.

The number of inquiries had declined. And two or three bodies had been withdrawn from deep freeze because of rising costs. At that time, fourteen bodies were being stored in New Jersey and California. But it took three hundred dollars per year to keep the bodies at the required temperature of −320° F. The total cost of cryonic suspension was running to about twenty thousand dollars, which included the cost of the stainless-steel cylinder in which the body was kept.

But what about merely cooling us down a little? Scientists have known for years about the stickleback fish. When it lives in the subpolar regions, it takes years to become sexually mature. But when it lives in warmer water, it may become sexually mature in a few months. Then there is the sardine, which can live much longer in cold water than in warm.

If this were true for humans, however, Eskimos would live longer than the natives of Ecuador. The reason they don't, of course, is that humans have a constant body temperature, no matter where they live. And fish are cold-blooded.

Scientists have found, though, that if the human body temperature could be lowered by three degrees and maintained at that level, it would add as much as twenty years to our life span. And they have the drugs to do it.

The problem is that all body processes, not just aging, would slow down. That means physical speed, brain power, and digestion. We would live longer, but we wouldn't be as intelligent. Perhaps the secret is to develop a way to lower our temperature only during sleep. We don't have to be as smart then. On the other hand, this would still slow down our elimination of waste and building of tissue processes. A lot of work must be done if we want to live longer by being colder.

There is also a possibility that lowering the body temperatures of other mammals makes them healthier, too. Rats have been refrigerated to a temperature of 50° F – 59° F and then warmed up after twenty hours. Jean Giaja, a biologist, has found that many of these rats increased their heart strength. What if, in the future, tissues and organs could be removed from a human body and rejuvenated by refrigeration? What if they were then regrafted into the body? Might this not be a way of improving the human body piece by piece?

The technique of lowering the body temperature has

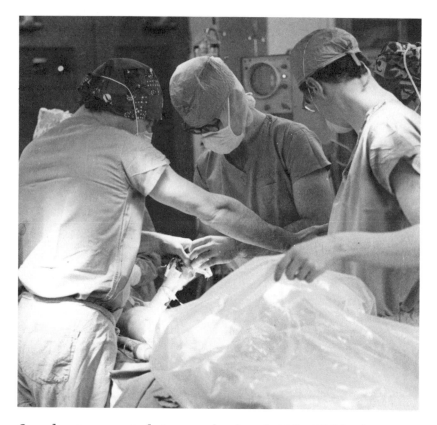

Open-heart surgery technique, as developed at The Children's Hospital Medical Center in Boston, starts with placing the child in a plastic bag.

also been used in open-heart surgery. This has even been done in an operation on a baby only thirty-six hours old.

After the baby was anesthetized, he was covered with a plastic blanket. Then the blanket was covered with cracked ice. Gradually his body cooled. And when it reached 77° F (98.6° F is normal), the operation began. The child was

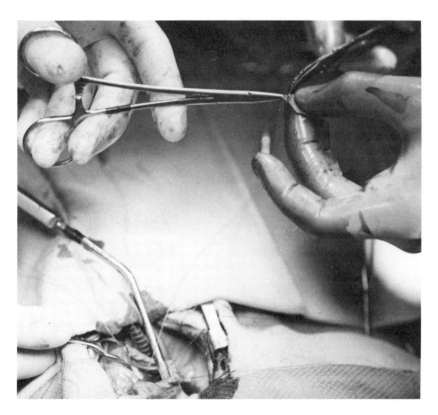

The patch for the child's heart is trimmed here by Dr. Castaneda.

hooked up with a heart-lung machine. The blood flowing into his body was cooled slowly until it was down to 68° F. Then the machine was turned off. The baby's heart was not beating and his blood was not circulating.

Now it was time to repair the heart. In less than an hour the operation was over. The pump was turned on again. Blood began to circulate. And as the blood became warmer and warmer, the baby's heart began to beat.

Dr. Aldo R. Castaneda, of Boston Children's Hospital Medical Center, has done more than eighty of these operations on very young children. He points out that there are more than eleven thousand babies born every year with heart defects. And more than four thousand of them need an operation during the first three months of their lives. But the usual equipment for open-heart surgery, the tubes and suction equipment, is too large for the tiny infant's chest—it blocks the surgeon's view.

One answer has been to perform a simpler operation while the child is young. But the child then has to have more surgery when he is older. A low-temperature operation, on the other hand, gets the job done all at once. And there is an additional advantage to low-temperature surgery. At normal temperatures, the brain is damaged if it goes without oxygenated blood for a matter of minutes. But with the patient's body temperature at 68° F, the surgeon has at least an hour to finish the operation; even though there is no blood circulating through the patient's brain, there is no brain damage.

There are other reasons for continuing with cryogenic research. Suppose that, after death, the characteristics of a great racehorse, a champion dog, or a human genius could still be passed on to future generations? This could become possible with the freezing of sperm. In the 1960s, Dr. S. J. Behrman of the University of Michigan reported success in the artificial insemination of human women, using male sperm that had been frozen for as long as eighteen months. Of the forty-four women who had received the sperm, eighteen became pregnant. None of the children showed defects attributable to the frozen sperm.

Farmers might be able to benefit from freezing techniques, too. In 1971, David Whittingham, of Sydney, Australia, was able to store living mice embryos in a freezer. The embryos were cooled to −110° F. After keeping them frozen for over thirty minutes, he raised the temperature and tested the embryos. Over two-thirds of them had survived and begun cell division again. He was then able to transplant the embryos to female mice and almost 70 percent of them developed to full term.

Whittingham pointed out that he was trying to find a method of preserving interesting mutant mice. But his experiments might lead to an acceptable way of shipping good farm stock all over the world in freezers. Perhaps the day might even come when the embryos of endangered species of animals might be saved in this way.

In 1973, a Hereford calf was born in Cambridge, England. The unusual thing about this animal was that it was the first large mammal to survive having been frozen as an embryo, thawed out, and implanted into a foster mother. It was born at the Agriculture Research Council's Unit of Reproductive Physiology and Biochemistry.

Some predictions were then made. Frozen embryos could be sent all over the world. This would be cheaper and less risky than sending the animals themselves. Also, many ova from a worthy cow could be fertilized at once and placed into other cows who have good mothering qualities. And cows who rarely reproduce twins could artificially be forced to do just that—increasing the population 100 percent when it seemed advisable.

So work goes on in freezing laboratory animals. At the Kobe Medical College in Japan, a cat brain was revived after it had been frozen at −4° F for almost seven months. Scientists had removed the blood from the brain and replaced the blood with an artificial solution. The solution contained liquid nitrogen. The brain was then removed from the cat's skull and stored in a bath of the same solution. When the brain was thawed out, it exhibited electrical activity, and a microscopic examination of the cells showed that they had an almost normal appearance.

In 1974, twelve dogs at Emory University in Atlanta were supercooled until they were clinically dead. For two hours, the animals were without any detectable heart or brain activity. Nor did they have any blood circulation or blood pressure.

An experiment with one of Dr. Vojin Popovic's ice-packed mice.

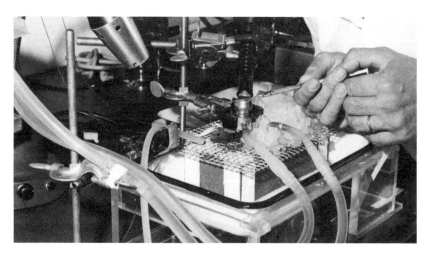

After two hours, the dogs were rewarmed to normal temperatures and all of their vital functions were restored. They continued to lead normal lives thereafter.

Dr. Vojin Popovic and his colleagues had gradually cooled the animals down to 40° F, eight degrees above freezing and fifty-eight degrees below normal. This was done by cooling both the animals' blood and their bodies. Popovic said that the dog tests marked the longest period on record of clinical death for large, warm-blooded, nonhibernating animals in which there was no permanent harm to the animals.

"The feat has important implications for man," Popovic said. "If we can do this with dogs, it can also be done with man. Think of what a boon it would be for surgeons to have several hours in which to complete a delicate operation instead of minutes, not having to worry about the patient's blood circulation or the possibility of brain damage.

"Without oxygen, the brain at normal temperatures will stay healthy only about five minutes. People (or animals) that go longer without oxygen and live are likely to exist in a 'vegetable' state. But when the body is cooled, metabolism slows down and almost all physiological functions of the body are changed. One effect of reduced metabolism has significance for space travel. Many scientists believe that when astronauts travel to distant planets on voyages lasting perhaps five years or more, they might be cooled into a hypothermic state and thus consume less food and oxygen. Also, their rate of aging would be slowed."

So we have come full circle. At least, scientists are still talking about the astronauts.

The Beginning of Life

For years, science-fiction writers have been telling about the world of the future. In this world, many of them have predicted, human egg cells will be fertilized in the laboratory. Embryos will be permitted to develop depending on whether or not they have the characteristics that the people in power want them to have.

This is not a happy idea for most of us. But there may come a day when such an arrangement is possible. So we had better consider the problem.

Almost ten years ago, Dr. Teh Ping Lin, of the University of California School of Medicine in San Francisco, announced the results of one of his experiments. He had injected tiny amounts of liquids into mice eggs. The liquid was bovine globulin, a protein found in blood plasma. Then he transferred the eggs into foster mice mothers' wombs. Some of the eggs grew into normal embryos, in spite of the fact that no sperm had touched them and they had not been fertilized.

Similar experiments had been done before on animals such as frogs. But Dr. Lin's experiment was an example of the development of an unfertilized egg, a process called parthenogenesis, in a mammal.

At about the same time, Dr. R. G. Edwards, of the Physiological Laboratory at the University of Cambridge, in England, described some of his experiments. He had taken some eggs from the ovaries of sixteen women. These women suffered from various disorders that made it necessary to surgically remove their ovaries. Edwards was able to get, on the average, fifteen immature eggs from each of the women.

He then placed the eggs in a nutrient solution, and they continued to develop just as they would have done in the human body. That is, they reached the state of maturity in which they could have been fertilized. The laboratory production of fertilized human eggs had become a possibility.

Carry that idea one step further and it would seem that it might be possible for a woman to have a child even though she had had her ovaries removed. If her eggs were saved, they might be fertilized in a test tube by her husband's sperm and replaced in her uterus. Then the fertilized egg could develop into a normal baby.

Dr. Edwards suggested that in the future his techniques could be used in several ways. Suppose that a woman produced normal eggs that were blocked in the fallopian tubes, the ducts that carry the eggs from the ovaries to the uterus. The eggs could be removed surgically, fertilized with the husband's sperm, and replaced in the wife's uterus. Or, if the woman were unable to produce eggs, the husband's sperm could be used to fertilize another egg from another woman, and this egg could be placed in his wife's womb to develop into an embryo.

Of course, there are questions to be answered. What about the eggs that are not chosen? Will murder have been committed when some eggs are allowed to die? Who will make the choice between these possible human beings? Who will say how many girls and how many boys should be born? Who will be the person to select the egg donor?

In 1972, the American Medical Association, worried about these questions, published an editorial in its *Journal of the American Medical Association.* It called for a stop to experiments involving implantation of fertilized eggs and fetuses into human uteruses. The organization felt that the many ethical problems raised by this type of research should be solved before continuing the experiments. Most people would agree with that.

However, in July of 1974, an announcement was made at the annual meeting of the British Medical Association. Dr. Douglas Bevis, of Leeds University in England, reported that three children had been born during the previous eighteen months as the result of some startling medical work. But he would not identify the scientists who had done the work.

The eggs of the mothers of these children had been removed and fertilized in laboratory dishes. Then the fertilized eggs had been reimplanted in their wombs. These were really the world's first test-tube babies. This kind of work was not new. As long ago as 1936, J. Jolly of the Collège de France was able to keep rat embryos and guinea pig embryos alive in a culture medium long enough so that their hearts began to pump blood. But the Leeds experiment was the first one with humans.

Many people were outraged for several reasons. Most

critics agreed that there was danger involved. And they were not talking about the obvious ethical problems concerning the morality of performing such experiments. No, they were disturbed by the possibility that the eggs might be damaged in the laboratory, and the resulting children would be abnormal. For this reason, critics felt it was wrong to carry out these experiments. They would not want to be responsible for the crippling and possible death of an infant, they said.

After three days of questioning, Bevis admitted that he had participated in the research. But he still refused to identify the other members of his team or the patients involved. The furor had been so great and the reactions against the research so violent that he wanted to protect the other people involved.

Scientists in the United States were asked about this type of experimentation. Some of them admitted that they were working on the fertilization of human ova in the laboratory. But they pointed out that they had no intention of trying to reimplant these fertilized eggs in humans. They said that there was a federal law against that kind of research.

Bevis later said that he was going to give up his own research. He was sickened by the publicity and incensed when a British newspaper offered him the English-pound equivalent of $120,000 for his personal story of the research.

The question still remains. Who makes the decision as to which fertilized egg lives and which dies?

But in the meantime, a lot of work has been done with cattle. The problem that cattle raisers have to face is that each of their prize cows can give birth to only about six or seven young during their lifetimes.

So cows have been given drugs that make them produce a large number of eggs. Then these eggs are fertilized inside the cow and removed shortly thereafter. Healthy-looking fertilized eggs are identified under the microscope and put into the uteruses of ordinary cows serving as foster mothers. That means that the prize cow is no longer pregnant, but she has many offspring developing in other cows and shortly can be used again to produce more eggs.

Hundreds of calves in the United States and Canada, as well as in England and Japan, have been born in this way.

Scientists are also working on the problem of determining the sex of an unborn child. For centuries there have been suggestions about how to pick the sex of the unborn.

Some people said that a boy would be born if his mother drank a mixture of wine and lion's blood. Others said that if the marriage bed pointed from north to south, a boy would be born. The ancient Greek philosopher, Parmenides, suggested that the wife lie on her right side to ensure a baby boy. In parts of Germany, it was believed that if the husband's ax was left in the house, a boy would be born. If he left it in the barn, the baby would be a girl.

But the fact still remains that it is the husband's sperm that determines the sex of the child. And perhaps an explanation is necessary.

The human body cell (but not the sex cells, the eggs and sperm) has forty-six chromosomes. These are threadlike bodies in the nucleus of the cell. Located on the chromosomes are the genes, the regions of the chromosome that govern hereditary traits such as height, hair and eye color, and intelligence.

The forty-six chromosomes are really twenty-three pairs of matching chromosomes. Each member of the pair contains genes that govern the same trait, but not necessarily in the same way. For example, a person may have a gene for blue eyes on one of the chromosomes, and a gene for brown eyes on the matching chromosome. But the person will have brown eyes, because the gene for brown eyes is dominant over the gene for blue eyes and blots out that gene.

Remember that every one of the human body cells has the same genetic makeup. But when it comes to forming sex cells, the sperm and the egg, a rather complicated process of cell division takes over. The result is that the sperm and the egg have only twenty-three chromosomes each, one from each pair that is found in the body cells. When fertilization occurs, the twenty-three chromosomes from the sperm align with the twenty-three from the egg. This results in a new mixture containing half the traits from the mother and half from the father. This is the same makeup as is found in the future body cells of the individual.

But now let us look at sex determination. Twenty-two of the twenty-three pairs of chromosomes in the body cells carry the genes for the same traits and are the same size. The exception is the pair called the X and Y chromosomes.

In 1891, a biologist named Henking was studying the sex cells of an insect, *Pyrrhocoris*. He noticed that the egg cells seemed to have one more chromosome than some of the sperm cells when they paired during fertilization. He called this extra female chromosome the X chromosome. All of the

Male Cell   Female Cell

A highly simplified diagram showing sex cell formation in the human. Left, the male cell contains forty-four chromosomes in twenty-two pairs, plus the X and Y. It produces sperm with one chromosome from each pair. Each sperm has twenty-two chromosomes plus either an X or a Y. Right, the female cell contains forty-four chromosomes in twenty-two pairs, plus a pair of Xs. Only one egg is actually produced by this cell. That egg contains twenty-two chromosomes, one from each pair, plus an X.

44
+
XY

44
+
XX

Egg

22
+
X

22
+
Y

22
+
X

Sperm

When human fertilization occurs, there is a fifty-fifty chance that an X-bearing sperm will fertilize the egg (all eggs contain the X chromosome), and a fifty-fifty chance that a Y-bearing sperm will fertilize the egg. The result will be either a girl, with twenty-two pairs of chromosomes plus two Xs, or a boy, with twenty-two pairs of chromosomes plus an X and a Y.

44
+
XX

44
+
XY

Female
Fertilized
Egg

Male
Fertilized
Egg

A *diagram showing the formation of sperm and eggs in the fruit fly. The fruit fly is shown because its cells have only four pairs of chromosomes. Left, the female cell produces two eggs containing one chromosome from each pair. Each egg contains an X chromosome. Right, the male cell produces two sperm containing one chromosome from each pair. But half of the sperm will have an X chromosome and half will have a Y. There is fifty-fifty chance, therefore, of either sex resulting from fertilization.*

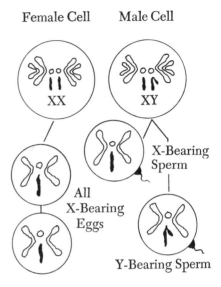

Female Cell   Male Cell

XX   XY

X-Bearing Sperm

All X-Bearing Eggs

Y-Bearing Sperm

1	2	3		4	5	XX
6	7	8	9	10	11	12
13	14	15		16	17	18
19	20				21	22

A diagram of the twenty-three pairs of chromosomes in the body cells of the human female. Notice that there are twenty-two pairs plus two X chromosomes. The male body cell would contain the same chromosomes except that it would have only one X, plus one Y. The diagram was made from a karyotype, which is a magnified pictorial arrangement of chromosomes.

egg cells had an X chromosome, but only half of the sperm cells had it.

An American scientist named McClung thought that this chromosome might have something to do with sex determination. That is, it might control whether the offspring would be male or female.

But it wasn't until 1910 that an important fact was discovered about the sex cells in humans. It had been thought that the female sex cell, the egg, had twenty-two chromosomes plus one X chromosome, and the male sex cell, the sperm, had only twenty-two chromosomes. But with the development of better microscopes, it was discovered that the X chromosome in the egg cell did pair up with another chromosome in the sperm. But this male chromosome, called the Y chromosome, was so small that it had been overlooked. So egg cells have twenty-two chromosomes plus an X chromosome, and male sex cells have twenty-two chromosomes plus a Y chromosome.

Then it was found that in many organisms the male body cells had both an X and a Y chromosome. But in the female body cells, there were two Xs and no Ys. The mystery was solved. Whether a child is a male or a female depends on the father. Remember we are talking about only one pair of chromosomes. Most human characteristics come from the other twenty-two pairs; only a few come from the X and Y because they are outnumbered. It works like this.

Human females have two Xs in their body cells. So when their sex cells, their eggs, are formed, every last one of them will contain one X. The male, on the other hand, has an X and a Y pair of chromosomes in his body cells. So when his sex cells, the sperm, are formed, the chances are about fifty-fifty that any one sperm cell will contain an X. And, of course, chances are also about fifty-fifty that a sperm cell will contain a Y.

If the sperm with an X chromosome fertilizes the female egg, which always has an X chromosome, the result of the pairing will be XX, or a female offspring. If the sperm with a Y chromosome fertilizes the egg, the result will be XY, or a male child.

You can see that sex is determined in humans during the process of fertilization, and nothing can be done about it. And you can also see that the chances are just about even as to which sex the baby will be.

If the human male wants to brag about the fact that the female has no control over the sex of the young, let him. But one thing must be pointed out. Apparently the Y chromosome contained in the sperm has no genes on it. So males inherit characteristics from the genes on the chromosome they get from their mothers. Remember, however, that the characteristics we are talking about now are only found in one pair of chromosomes. There are still twenty-two other pairs with many other traits on them.

Even if a trait carried by a gene in the X chromosome is recessive and could have been overcome by a dominant gene on another X chromosome (as was mentioned about brown eye genes being dominant over blue eye genes on another chromosome), the male offspring would inherit the recessive trait because there is no dominant gene on the Y chromosome to mask it. Therefore, whatever genes are contained in the X chromosome donated by the mother will show up in the boy babies.

The mother may not even show this trait herself. She has two Xs, and a recessive trait on one of them may be masked by a dominant gene on the other. Half of her sex cells will have the dominant gene and half will have the recessive gene. So the chances are fifty-fifty that her male babies will show the recessive trait. Remember, males have no dominant gene to mask the recessive gene.

As far as her girl children are concerned, the chances are, of course, that half of them will have the recessive gene, too. But it is probable that they will not show the trait, since the X chromosome that comes from the father often will have a dominant gene to mask the recessive gene from the mother.

So, the sex-linked genes on the pair of sex chromosomes all come to the son from his mother, while both mother and father give sex-linked genes to their daughters. Let's take an example.

Sufferers from hemophilia have blood that will not clot. That means that if they are cut, they will continue to bleed. And without medical attention, they could bleed to death very easily.

Hemophilia is a semirare disease. The problem is that it is inherited. Luckily, the gene for the disease is recessive. However, it is sex linked.

Hemophilia is hardly ever present in women. The gene is on the X chromosome, and it is recessive. So, even if a woman carries it on one of her Xs, she will probably have a dominant clotting gene on her other X and therefore will not suffer from the disease. Of course, half of her sex cells will carry the hemophilia gene. That means that there is a fifty-fifty chance that her son will have the disease.

There is also a fifty-fifty chance that her daughters will carry the hemophilia gene, but they will probably not show the disease. But if the daughter has inherited the hemophilia gene from her mother, the daughter's male offspring will have a fifty-fifty chance of showing the disease. So the daughters, even though they don't show the disease, may pass it along to their children.

There are many other sex-linked traits that are passed on in the same way. And quite a few of them are undesirable. Baldness is one, and so are a type of muscular dystrophy and a type of diabetes.

Let's get back to determining the sex of the unborn child. It is all a matter of being able to separate the X-bearing sperm cells from the Y-bearing ones. If this becomes possible, a moral problem will arise. Does the scientist eliminate all of the X-bearing sperm cells if the father is a hemophiliac? This would stop the disease from being passed on to his children, but is it ethical to force the mother to bear only sons?

Several ways of separating the X-carrying sperm from the Y-carrying sperm have been tried. The Y chromosome is smaller than the X chromosome, and so it is lighter in weight. That means that Y-carrying sperm could be separated from X-carrying sperm by spinning them on a centrifuge. The heavier sperm would end up at the bottom of the test tube with the lighter ones, the Y sperm, above them. But many of the sperm might be damaged.

In 1972, Dr. A. M. Roberts, of Guy's Hospital in London, observed human sperm's swimming motions. His discovery was that the Y sperm moved through the fluid faster than the X sperm.

A German scientific team placed separate sperm, both X and Y, in a solution that contained some albumin. This albumin was similar to the white of an egg. The albumin was denser than seminal fluid and so it was more difficult for sperm to swim through it. The researchers were able to isolate a group of sperm that was 85 percent Y sperm just by capturing the fastest swimmers.

The last step is yet to be taken. That is, the selection of sperm of a specific sex for implantation into a human female. But no one knows whether or not sperm that have gone through this racecourse are still capable of fertilizing a human egg. However, rabbit sperm that have had the same treatment have been found to be fertile.

Is this a good thing? Male versus female births are about equal now. But what if this balance were upset, let's say, in favor of boys? There would be several men to each woman, and what would that do to our current system of marriage? Then, too, 90 percent of all crimes are committed by men. Would the rate of crime go up with more men than women in the world? Also, would sex selection lead to more sex discrimination?

Suppose that people could select the sex of their unborn children. Would they pick boys or girls? A study reported in 1974 was conducted by Charles Westoff of Princeton University and Ronald Rindfuss of the University of Wisconsin.

They had interviewed nearly six thousand American

women. It turned out that most of them would prefer a first-born child to be a boy. But if they were going to have a second child, they would want a girl, to balance the family. So the scientists claimed that even if the sex of the child could be picked, there would be no significant change in the national sex ratio at birth of 105 boys to 100 girls.

However, the researchers were cautious. Husbands' votes had not been requested. And the ratio might be thrown off because of the increasing trend toward one-child families.

7

The Future of Life

Before we know where we are going, we must know where we have been. The last two centuries have produced more changes in our lives than all of the previous two million years that man has been on the earth.

Take life expectancy. It has been estimated that in the first six million human generations, the length of life for the average person was twenty to thirty years. Just six generations later, the average life span had tripled. Most of this increase was caused by medical discoveries that permitted us to prevent and cure diseases more efficiently.

These medical discoveries also reduced the rate of infant mortality. Since fewer children died, fewer children had to be born in order to keep the farm or the store going. At the time of the Revolutionary War, families of twenty children were not unusual. Today, the average family in this country has about 2.1 children.

Technology has changed our lives, too. The automobile and other machines have turned us into a nation of movers. The average American changes his address every five years. And we are a nation with a lot of free time. Our jobs have gone from an eighty-hour week to a forty-or-less-hour week. We retire at an ever-decreasing age — retirement was unknown two hundred years ago, and now, many people retire in their fifties.

Women are working outside the home more than at any time in history. Thirty-five years ago, only 17 percent of the women in this country worked outside the home. Today, with the ever-increasing economic drain on families and a greater demand for women workers in industry, nearly half of the women in the country are in the labor force. It is obvious that our ideas about the family are changing.

So are our attitudes about reproduction. The Abbé Lazzaro Spallanzani was the first to succeed in the artificial insemination of toads and frogs in 1789. He was later successful in doing the same thing with dogs. Spallanzani's friend, Charles Bonnet, commented on this experimentation: "This is one of the greatest innovations that has been presented to naturalists and philosophers since the creation of the world. Nothing can be more accurate nor more firmly proven, nothing as beautiful or as new, as this experiment."

But just 160 years later, semen was being successfully frozen and thawed out. Since then, there has been a revolution in animal husbandry and even in human reproduction. It is estimated that one in every 150 human babies born in this country is the product of artificial insemination. And there are about twenty-five human-sperm banks in this country alone.

Frozen embryos are new, and there is a possibility that in the future, fertilized human eggs will be frozen and later transferred to a substitute mother. Embryo transplants in animals have been performed for more than twenty years.

It may soon be possible to choose the sex of an unborn child before the fertilization of the egg. And scientists are working on the development of a human womb. It is estimated that this will be a reality by the turn of the next century. The Institute for the Future predicts that by 1985, it will be possible to create a living human embryo from an unfertilized egg.

We haven't come much closer to being able to manufacture artificial life in the last few years. As far back as 1962, a startling announcement was reported. It was said that scientists had succeeded in making viruses out of chemicals.

Dr. George W. Cochran of Utah State University, and a team of scientists led by Dr. Sam G. Wildman and Dr. Young Tai Kim of the University of California, Los Angeles, reported that they had produced a virus in a test tube. Cochran worked independently from Wildman and Kim, but the two groups came to the same conclusion.

In their investigations, they injected a nucleic acid into test tubes containing inert chemicals. This acid was the same type as can be found in the virus that causes the tobacco mosaic disease. The scientists felt that the nucleic acid organized the chemicals into viruses.

But had they really created life? In the first place, these experiments may not have produced a new virus. They might have produced a kind of virus protein out of protein and nucleic acid. Perhaps the materials came from an already existing virus and were not created by the researchers. And, there are many scientists who do not consider viruses living things, since there are several life processes that they do not engage in. So the creation of life seems a long way off.

Of all the developments with possibilities for the future, the one that seems to have caught the public's fancy the most is *cloning*. A clone is a pure line of cells. That is, all of the cells in the clone are genetically identical. The word itself means *cutting*, and it was first used by botanists to describe nonsexual reproduction, as when a cutting from a certain plant grows to form a new plant. Obviously, the new plant has exactly the same genetic makeup as the plant from which the cutting came.

For centuries, farmers have been growing potatoes by cloning. All they had to do was cut the potato into pieces, each containing an eye, and plant them. Then, with luck, a new potato would grow from each planting. And the new potato, since it was grown from body cells and not sex cells, would have the same genes as the parent.

In 1952, Drs. Robert Briggs and Thomas King were successful in cloning leopard frogs at the Institute for Cancer Research, in Philadelphia. First, they took fertilized leopard frog's eggs out of the female. The nuclei of these cells were surgically removed and replaced with the nuclei of cells from a single leopard frog embryo. The result was a clone of tadpoles. All of them were genetically identical to the frog embryo that had supplied the nuclei.

A hornet's nest was stirred up. What if humans could be cloned? Just imagine a large population of genetically identical twins!

Those who favor the development of this technique point out that an Einstein or a Beethoven or a Catfish Hunter could have been reproduced exactly, if we had had the techniques to do it available during their lifetimes. Of course, we are still a long way from perfecting those techniques. Those who oppose cloning are concerned with the ethical problems of who would be chosen to be reproduced and who would make that decision.

There are those who think that cloning of humans would lead to the extinction of the human race. And they may be right. If everyone were exactly alike, there would be few adaptations to the environment as it changed. The result might be that human beings would disappear, just like the mammoth and the tyrannosaurus.

However, we still do not know how to clone human beings. Human eggs do not normally become fertilized outside the body, as do frog eggs. Human eggs do not develop in pond water, either, and no one has yet been able to reproduce the human uterus in all its complexity. Human eggs are also much smaller than frog eggs, so microsurgery would be difficult.

Some people are worried about the implications of all this scientific research. And there is reason for worry. Here is what Jean Rostand, a French scientist, once imagined the human of the future as saying:

> I was born of stock chosen and irradiated by neutrons; they chose my sex and I was born of a mother who was not mine; during my development, I had been given injections of hormones and DNA; I have benefitted from treatment which superactivated the cortex of my brain; after my birth, tissue grafts were made to improve my intellectual development, and even now I submit myself every year to a course of maintenance treatment in order to keep my mind in good shape and my instincts at optimum level. I

have no reason to be discontented with my body, my sex, or my life, but who am I?

Is this the kind of alienation we can expect from future generations? Where are we really headed? Dr. Robert T. Francoeur, professor of embryology, bio-ethics, and human sexuality, at Fairleigh Dickinson University in Madison, New Jersey, has made some predictions about the scientific world of the future.

He believes that we have now, or soon will have, thirteen startling items to cope with. Simply put, these are:

1. There will be inexpensive, non-habit-forming drugs that can change our personalities.
2. Primitive life will be created in the laboratory.
3. An artificial heart will be developed.
4. The rejection problem will be solved and transplants will become more common.
5. A brain transplant will become a possibility.
6. Genes in unborn babies will be changed, perhaps to eliminate defects.
7. A way may be found to permit humans to grow new organs and limbs.
8. Electrical stimulation of the brain will be used to help in cases of spastic paralysis and brain damage.
9. Our life span will be increased to 120 years through the use of chemicals.
10. Human life will be maintained for years through cryogenic freezing.
11. We will be able to control the body's development to increase size and intelligence.

12. Through electricity, brain communication will be improved, possibly leading to control of telepathic messages.

13. Drugs will be developed to raise intelligence and improve memory, learning, and perception.

The problem is, what choices do we make? When these things are developed, will we use them to benefit humanity and protect our future as moral people? No one can answer these questions, as any student of history can testify.

But the decisions cannot be left up to any one person or any one group, whether the person or group is involved in politics, medicine, religion, or law. No, the decisions must be made by all the people.

As Dr. Francoeur points out, "An old proverb warns that without a vision of where they are going, the people will perish. At no time in human history has that proverb been truer to the mark, or fairer in its warning."

Finally, perhaps we should all keep in mind the warning that was given by the French philosopher, Guy Durandin:

> With the help of science, woman will no longer receive her child; she will order it with masculine or feminine sex, blue or brown eyes, blond, brown, or chestnut hair. All that will need to be done will be to delete inapplicable words on the Laboratory's order form. We still have a tendency to defend ourselves against such notions, to treat them ironically, but we should try to understand why they trouble us. It is simply that they lead to the negation of human nature. It is not possible for us to wish for anything except from a natural basis which we accept as "given," which does not depend on us, and which we cannot alter. If man can be modified at will, if there is no longer such a thing as human nature, there can no longer be a human destiny, and we shall have reached the point of absurdity. If human

nature no longer exists, then neither do good nor evil; human desire would be meaningless, as it would be the desire of nobody.

All of this may sound quite negative. But let's consider a few things before we get too depressed.

Hardly anyone would argue with the success that modern scientists have achieved in prolonging healthy lives, in reducing infant mortality, or in helping the handicapped function more normally. Where we find disagreement is when we consider such things as freezing or transplanting human embryos, selecting the sex of a future human being, or defining death in a moral and ethical way.

But the ray of hope shining through all of this is the fact that now, more than ever before, scientists are using their consciences. And the general public is aware that problems exist.

Time was when people stood in awe of science. They believed what they were told. Nuclear reactors were safe. All drugs were thoroughly tested before they were used on humans. The supersonic transport airplane was a boon to mankind.

Now there is a healthy suspicion of scientific breakthroughs. And the scientists themselves are paying more attention to the human implications of their work. Indeed, they are sometimes the first to point out the bad effects of their discoveries. With an alert general public and a concerned scientific community, there is hope that the pessimists will be proved wrong and that the world of the future will be a healthy one, rather than a planet populated by computer-run men and women.

Bibliography

ALLEN, TOM. *The Quest: A Report on Extraterrestrial Life*. Philadelphia: Chilton Co., 1965.

AYLESWORTH, THOMAS G. *The Alchemists: Magic Into Science*. Reading, Mass.: Addison-Wesley Publishing Co., 1973.

BUTLER, S. T., and RAYMOND, ROBERT. *Introduction to Modern Medicine*. Frontiers of Science, 2. Garden City, New York: Doubleday & Co., Anchor Press, 1974.

COLE, JOANNA, and EDMONDSON, MADELEINE. *Twins: The Story of Multiple Births*. New York: William Morrow & Co., 1972.

HANDLER, PHILIP, ed. *Biology and the Future of Man*. New York: Oxford University Press, 1970.

HELLMAN, HAL. *Biology in the World of the Future*. New York: M. Evans & Co., 1971.

KLEIN, AARON E. *Threads of Life: Genetics from Aristotle to DNA*. Garden City, New York: Natural History Press, 1970.

KLEIN, STANLEY. *The Final Mystery*. Garden City, New York: Doubleday & Co., 1974.

LONGMORE, DONALD. *Spare-Part Surgery: The Surgical Practice of the Future*. Garden City, New York: Doubleday & Co., 1968.

McCULLOCH, G. L. *Man Alive*. London: Aldus Books, 1967.

ROSTAND, JEAN and DELAUNAY, ALBERT, eds. *Man of Tomorrow*. Encyclopedia of the Life Sciences, vol. 8. Garden City, New York: Doubleday & Co., 1966.

ROTHMAN, MILTON A. *The Cybernetic Revolution: Thought and Control in Man and Machine*. New York: Franklin Watts, 1972.

SAGAN, CARL. *The Cosmic Connection: An Extraterrestrial Perspective*. Garden City, New York: Doubleday & Co., Anchor Press, 1973.

SIMON, SEYMOUR. *About Your Heart*. New York: McGraw-Hill Book Co., 1974.

Index

absorption, 31, 35

aging: current interest in, 11

Albertus Magnus, 22–4

alchemists. *See* alchemy

alchemy, 11–25: and basilisk, 23–4; discoveries in, 12; and elixir of life, 14–17, 21; and gold, 12–13, 15, 24; and homunculus, 21–5; and philosopher's stone, 12, 14–16, 22, 24; and religion, 14–15, 18, 22, 24; and rulers, 14. *See also* Albertus Magnus; Arnold of Villanova; Paracelsus

Alejew, L. S., 48–9

ALG (antilymphocytic globulin), 77

ALS (antilymphocytic serum), 77–8

ameba, 33, 38

American Medical Association, 96

amino acids, 27–8, 30, 32

amputees: prostheses for. *See* artificial limbs; myoelectric control in prosthetics

amylase, 30

anaerobic organisms, 32

animal husbandry: advances in, 91, 97–8

anorganic bone, 74

antibodies: and transplants, 69–72, 74, 77–8, 81

anticoagulants. *See* artificial blood part

antigen: definition of, 70

antilymphocytic globulin. *See* ALG

antilymphocytic serum. *See* ALS

anti-rejection drugs, 68

Aquinas, Thomas, 24

arc lamp, 46–7

Arnold of Villanova, 17–18

arteries: grafting, 73; plastic, 43

arthritis: and artificial joints, 47–8

artificial blood part, 45

artificial insemination, 90, 109; and frozen sperm, 90; of laboratory animals, 109

artificial life: creation of, 25, 110–11, 113. *See also* homunculus

artificial limbs, 42–4, 51–3. *See also* prosthetics

artificial organs, 43. *See also* prosthetics; *and under names of specific organs*

assimilation, 32–3, 35

atheriosclerosis: and kidney dialysis care, 63

atmosphere: earth's early, 27

autografts, 68, 71: bone, 73–4

Avicenna, 20

Bacon, Roger, 14

baldness. *See* sex-linked traits

Balmer, L., 54

Barnard, Dr. Christiaan, 74, 78–9

Barraquer, Dr. José, 73

basilisk, 23–4

bat sonar instrument, 53–4

Behrman, Dr. S. J., 90

PRINTED IN U.S.A.